D0118251

EMERGENCY
PREPAREDNESS
The Right Way

By
Howard Godfrey

ii

ISBN: 1-4392-4478-2

Copies of the book may be ordered
From
Howard Godfrey
P.O. Box 3214, Bowman, Ca. 95604

Dedication
This book is dedicated to my wife
Bonnie, who has been extremely helpful
with research and very patient during
my hours on the computer and to my
extended family especially Nancy, who
have been supportive, offered
suggestions and helped with the proof
reading. Also to the Freeze Dry Guy
who has provided me with information
and support.

TABLE OF CONTENTS

EMERGENCY PREPAREDNESS

The Right Way

Introduction

Due to the state of the world financial markets, threats of terrorism and war, more and more people are beginning to store food and other necessities of life. It is a project that requires knowledge and access to resource materials. Without these, it is very easy to waste your time and money.

I have read most of the books that are commonly available and have been very disappointed in them. Most of them are incomplete, deal largely with recipes or are overly complicated. Because of my studies, I have decided to write this book.

This book deals with the food and necessities that the average family would require in an emergency. I will not attempt to write about firearms, self-defense, NBC warfare (nuclear, biological or chemical) or medical care in any detail. These are all very comprehensive subjects and numerous good books are already available. In the Reference Section, you will find all the references you need to become knowledgeable in these areas.

I have attempted to prioritize the items you need to acquire, to keep the lists simple and to provide methods to improvise where possible. By utilizing these methods and rotating supplies, you will be able to reduce your costs and prevent waste.

Good luck on your storage.

Chapter 1 - Planning and other Random Thoughts

While on the fire department, I responded to a fire in an elementary school. The fire did a significant amount of damage to the classrooms and there was a lot of smoke and flame. I remember being amazed at the way the children had responded. All the children were out of the building and lined up on the playground with no panic or confusion. This made me realize the importance of planning. The fire drills at that school had paid off.

The same principle applies to preparedness; you have to plan ahead. What are you preparing for? What are the hazards in your neighborhood? Are you in a flood plain, an earthquake zone or a fire area? Do you live near a railroad track, a major highway (chemical spills) or military base? Do you live in the city, an urban area or rural area? Are you planning for terrorism, nuclear war, EMP (electro magnetic pulse) or a pandemic? Do you fear the government? These are just part of the questions you have to ask yourself as you begin planning.

Most of us do not have the financial resources to prepare for every eventuality. It is important to decide what events are most likely to affect you. Food, water and first aid supplies are some of the items that are common to every scenario. Concentrate on them first. After acquiring the basics, branch out into the areas that concern your special needs.

This book talks about food, water, medical supplies and 72-hour kits (bug out bags). It also gives some recipes and tips to make your life a little easier. No book can possibly cover everything about preparedness, which is why it is important that you continue your studies. Upon finishing this book, you will understand that preparedness is about more than material things, it is a state of mind, it is the knowledge you carry in your head. There is a reference list of books, web sites and suppliers at the end of this book. When you complete this book, keep studying, planning and practicing what you have learned.

Firearms-I know individuals who put their primary emphasis on firearms and ammunition and others who have none, but put their trust in God. Personally, I believe that if you can legally possess firearms, you should. If you make the decision to obtain firearms there are a few basic rules you should follow: only own legal weapons, practice with your weapons and learn to use them safely. Store them where they are protected from theft and children. In the Reference Section at the rear of the book, you will find books, suppliers and schools that will help you.

Nuclear explosion - First, understand that nuclear warfare is survivable with a little luck, skill and training. I believe that eventually there will be a nuclear incident in the United States. The incident will be caused by either terrorists or a foreign power. It will be either a dirty bomb or a nuclear explosion. <u>Nuclear War Survival Skills</u>, by Cresson H Kearny is in my opinion the best book ever written on this subject. Get a copy of this book, read it and learn how to protect yourself.

EMP attacks are generated when a nuclear weapon is detonated at altitudes a few dozen miles or higher above the Earth's surface. The explosion of even a small warhead would produce a set of electromagnetic pulses that interact with the Earth's atmosphere and the Earth's magnetic field.

 "These electromagnetic pulses propagate from the burst point of the nuclear weapon to the line of sight on the Earth's horizon, potentially covering a vast geographic region doing so simultaneously, moreover, at the speed of light," said Dr. Lowell Wood, acting chairman of the commission appointed by Congress to study the threat. "For example, a nuclear weapon detonated at an altitude of 400 kilometers (124 miles) over the central United States would cover, with its primary electromagnetic pulse, the entire continent of the United States and parts of Canada and Mexico."

"The electromagnetic field pulses produced by weapons designed and deployed with the intent to produce EMP have a high likelihood of damaging electrical power systems, electronics and information systems upon which any reasonably advanced society, most specifically including our own, depend vitally," Wood said. "Their effects on systems and infrastructures dependent on electricity and electronics could be sufficiently ruinous as to qualify as catastrophic to the American nation."

No one seems to know exactly what would survive. Cars with points should survive; newer cars with electronic ignition probably would not.

Unprotected computers may not survive. Small electronics can be protected by a Faraday cage, which is an enclosed ungrounded metal container. The contents must be insulated from touching the metal sides of the container. A microwave oven is a good example of a Faraday cage. The microwave oven does not have to be in working condition. An old microwave with the cord cut off should protect small electronic items from EMP.

I have not attempted to explain EMP and Faraday cages in detail. For detailed information on grounding large systems, get a copy of Army Technical Manual 5-690.

Earthquakes, floods, **natural disasters** - If you follow the preparedness guidelines given in this book and use a little common sense you will be prepared for these disasters. Make plans for the types of natural disasters likely to occur near your residence. Do not build in flood plains and try to stay off earthquake faults. Stay away from main highways and railroad tracks because they can transport hazardous materials.

Keep a pair of shoes near your bed. One of the most common injuries in an earthquake is cut feet. This is the result of people panicking and running through broken glass and debris to exit buildings.

Groups can consist of family, friends, churches, neighbors or just individuals with a common goal. In all cases, you face similar problems.

Make a Group Emergency Plan. Your group may not be together when disaster strikes, so it is important to know how to contact one another and to know where you will meet.

Plan rally points where your group will gather, both within and outside of your neighborhood.

It may be easier to make a long distance phone call than to call across town, so have an out-of-area contact number. If the phones are working, you can leave messages at the out-of-area phone number for other members of the group.

You may also want to inquire about emergency plans at daycare centers and schools your children attend. Know what the procedures are for picking up children from school.

Be sure to take into consideration any physical handicaps or other limitations members may have because of age and health.

In the process of organizing, a group, consider the skills and abilities of the members. Encourage members to develop new skills and learn from each other.

Retreats- a hideaway in the backcountry. I am not a big believer in retreats unless they are your permanent residence. Often retreats are located several hundred miles from where you normally live and work. It is easy to use all your resources to construct a retreat. Then when the time comes to evacuate to your retreat, you may find your route blocked because of martial law, civil disturbance, pandemic or other causes. Always have a plan and the supplies needed to shelter in place.

Urban versus rural -The situation we would all like to find ourselves in is out in the country with all our family, friends and supplies at a nice, safe, secure place off the grid with water and nice gardens. Unfortunately, this is a pipe dream for most of us; we will be trapped in the urban environment in which we normally reside.

A few guidelines for urban survival: Keep your preparations secret. Do not brag to neighbors, friends, etc. Know your neighborhood and neighbors. Know your local water sources, for example, fountains, ponds, water heaters and toilet tanks. In multi-story buildings, there are large volumes of water in the fire sprinkler system. In cold climates beware of antifreeze in fire sprinkler systems.

Do not run generators or show lots of light at night. Avoid attracting attention to yourself. Watch for like-minded people with whom you can ally. One of the biggest problems for people who live in rural areas will be refugees from the cities. They will be hungry and desperate.

In discussing preparedness with various groups, I always find someone who thinks they can go off into the woods and survive off the country. Invariably, this person has little hunting or survival experience and their opinion is based on survival books they have read. Most people who try this will lack the experience and equipment needed to succeed.

Hundreds, possibly thousands of people, may flee to the countryside seeking refuge. A good portion of these people will have little if any outdoor experience. Depending on the time of the year and the ground cover, their attempts at camping will result in wildfires. This group will include a small percentage of anarchists and pyromaniacs who may deliberately set fires. When you make your plans, consider the strong possibility of major unchecked wildfires that involve hundreds of thousands of acres.

Heating in an emergency - If you live in a cold climate, your best choice is a wood stove. A stove will provide heat, both for warmth and cooking. A propane or kerosene heater is your second choice; just make sure they are approved for indoor use. Keep in mind that it is easier to heat a small space.

In situations where people have been totally without heat in below freezing weather, they have survived by building a tent or shelter inside the house. In that small space a kerosene lantern or a candle will provide a surprising amount of heat. If there are several people, your combined body heat will make a big difference. If you use a candle or lantern, beware of fire.

Edible plants - Native Americans utilized many of the plants in your area for both food and medicinal purposes. Plant knowledge is an excellent method of supplementing your diet in an emergency. Many of the survival books published by the military and other sources are too general. They are designed for worldwide use. If you look in your local bookstores, check with the county agricultural department and local colleges, you should be able to find an edible plant book specific to your area. Spend a little time talking to older residents; they are often knowledgeable about the local plants and very willing to share information.

Communication - I recommend that you have equipment in the 2-meter band and a CB unit. This will provided you with short-range communication of approximately twenty to thirty miles. If the repeaters are still working in your area, the range is almost unlimited with a 2-meter radio. You need to learn how to operate your units and practice. A good idea is to find the local ARES (Amateur Radio Emergency Service) and join.

ARES's website states the following, "The Amateur Radio Emergency Service (ARES) consists of licensed amateurs who have voluntarily registered their qualifications and equipment for communications duty in the public service when disaster strikes. Every licensed amateur, regardless of membership in ARRL (Amateur Radio Relay league) or any other local or national organization is eligible for membership in ARES. The only qualification, other than possession of an Amateur Radio license, is a sincere desire to serve."

They are an excellent source of information and have books for sale on their website.

The new family channel radios have extended their ranges to between 20 and 30 miles. These radios work of AA batteries. They are inexpensive and user friendly. The down side is that they will not work with repeaters.

Psychology of Survival or Will You Eat a Rat?

"Will you eat a rat?" is a legitimate question. If your answer is no, you are not mentally prepared to survive. In parts of the world, rats are considered a delicacy. One of the first ideas that the military teaches about surviving in a prisoner of war camp is no matter how bad the food, never miss a meal. In a real survival situation when you are short of food, you have to eat anything and everything. A meal missed is calories you may never get back.

During World War 2 when rationing was tight and food was short, many Europeans ate roof hares (a euphemism for cats) and horses. The trick is to make up your mind ahead of time that you are a survivor.

Early in the Second World War, the Merchant Marine noticed that the average age of survivors from ships sinking was in the forties and fifties. Research showed that the younger, stronger men were giving up faster. This is why the Military pushes you to exceed your limits. Most of us never really have to find out what we are capable of doing.

Regardless of what equipment you have hidden away, it all comes down to you having the emotional stability, the determination and the knowledge to use it. You will die or become a burden on your friends or family if you become an emotional basket case.

I have a strong belief in God and feel that this gives me the spiritual strength to face adversity. Whatever system of beliefs or principles you follow, be sure that they are strong enough to sustain you. Remember, you are mentally and physically stronger than you think you are.

Chapter 2 - Water

Other than air, water is probably our most important survival need. In hot desert climates like the southwestern United States, you may require up to 2 gallons a day. I live in a more moderate area, but always plan on at least one gallon a day per person.

The amount and method of water storage you require depends on the following considerations:

Water sources - Do you have a well or readily available surface water? If you are on a well, do you have alternate sources of power to operate the well pump? If not, a simple method for getting water out of a deep well without electricity is shown below.

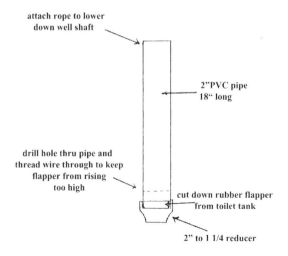

attach rope to lower down well shaft

2"PVC pipe 18" long

drill hole thru pipe and thread wire through to keep flapper from rising too high

cut down rubber flapper from toilet tank

2" to 1 1/4 reducer

Attach a rope to the PVC pipe and lower the bucket down the 4 to 6 inch well shaft, and let it sink into the water. The rubber flapper will act like a foot valve and rise up against the wires when it hits the water. This will allow the water to enter the pipe. When you start to pull it up, the weight of the water will push the rubber flapper down against the reducer and seal the bottom of the bucket.

Streams and surface water are not a safe source of drinking water. I live in a semi-rural area in which a lot of gold mining occurred. The miners used mercury in large quantities and water from the mines may be dangerous to your health. Be familiar with the history of what has occurred in your neighborhood.

Do not trust water from springs or mountain streams. There are many old wives' tales about beds of sand and gravel purifying water. The space between grains of sand is more than enough to let microscopic giardia lamblia parasites pass between them. Trust me, you do not want giardia. A young healthy friend of mine had it and lost 40 pounds in about three weeks!

Giardia and Cryptosporidium are two waterborne diseases that are often found in swimming pools and hot tubs as well as in rural settings. They are spread by human and animal feces and are hard to destroy.

Remember that during the Civil War more men died from diseases caused by unsanitary conditions than combat. Read the section on water purification later in this chapter.

Are you in a city, urban, or a rural environment? If you reside in a city or urban area, you are probably dependent on a municipal water system. In times of turmoil, they will not be reliable. Be aware of other sources of water in your neighborhood. For instance, rivers, streams, swimming pools or fountains can be useful sources of water during a crisis. As neighborhoods change, wells are capped and abandoned. An old timer may remember the location of one.

Contamination - Are there natural or man made contaminates in the water? One should ask this question before drinking it. Contaminates could include animal or human waste as well as chemicals. I have a stream across the street from my house. It is contaminated with animal waste. In an emergency, a large percentage of the population would not know how to deal with waste products and would contribute to the contamination. Washing clothes, dishes and bathing in available surface water are some examples. Assume that any water other than from a deep well is contaminated.

Ok, so how much water do you store? Figure a minimum of one gallon a day per person. This only includes drinking, cooking and very basic hygiene, such as washing dishes and brushing teeth.

Therefore, if you had a family of five and you decided you needed water for two weeks, 5x14 equals 70 gallons. In my opinion, this is an absolute minimum. To store 70 gallons of water is a lot easier then it sounds. You probably have 40 gallons in your hot water tank and several gallons in the toilet tanks. If you plan to use the water from the toilet tanks, do not add any cleaning materials or disinfectants to the tank water. At the first sign of an emergency shut off any connections to a municipal water system. The water in your pipes and water heater should be safe to drink. If you do not isolate your plumbing from the municipal water system, your water may become contaminated. Be sure to turn off the heat before draining a water heater.

How do you store water without spending lots of money? You can go to the local sporting goods store, and buy several 5-gallon containers. Of course, these are going to run you from $10 to $20 dollars each. If you have the money this is alright, but there are cheaper ways.

A friend of mine saves his two-liter soda bottles, washes them out and fills them with fresh water. He then throws them in the crawl space under his home. Two-liter soda bottles make excellent storage containers. These are strong, light and designed to hold liquids.

Everyday you throw away high quality storage containers, in particular juice and water bottles.

Beware of plastic milk containers, as these have a tendency to break down and the lids do not seal well. Bleach bottles have been recommended in the past; however, the current manufacturers of bleach do not recommend that they be used for water storage. Plastic containers that are marked PETE or PET are safe for use. Only food grade containers should be used. Do not use containers that have been used to store nonfood items. Plastic bottles are permeable and should not be stored near flammable liquids, pesticides, or other chemicals. They will pick up tastes and odors of chemicals and flammable liquids stored in close proximity.

Water has been stored in everything from waterbeds to canning jars. Beware of waterbeds, because they are not made of food grade plastic. They may contain dangerous chemicals. There are pros and cons to all methods. Fifty-five gallon barrels or other large containers are too heavy to carry and often require you to siphon or pump the water out. Inexpensive Hand pumps are available. You can improvise a siphon hose.

Fifteen and thirty gallon containers are a bit lighter and easier to move. They are used for the delivery of syrups to various food manufactures and restaurants. They can sometimes be found in surplus yards or purchased through the suppliers listed in the Reference Section. If you know a restaurant owner, check with them to see how they dispose of their containers.

Five-gallon containers are easier to carry, but remember, they weigh about 50 lbs each. If you have to walk to a water source, you can run a pole through the handle of one or more five-gallon containers and two people can share the weight. Water weighs 8.35 lbs to the gallon.

Glass jars are an effective way to store water; they are non-permeable and will not pick up bad tastes and odors. Remember to protect glass; it is easily broken in case of earthquake or other disasters.

A great place to store water bottles is in the available free space in your freezer. This makes your freezer more efficient and the ice helps to keep the food cold in case of a power failure.

Storing the water in the various types of containers is easy. First, be sure the containers are clean. Thoroughly wash all containers prior to filling. A sanitizing solution can be prepared by mixing 1 teaspoon of liquid chorine bleach (5 to 6% sodium hypochlorite) to 1 quart of water. Use only household bleach without thickeners, scents or additives. Second, if you have access to clean pure tap water from a chlorinated municipal water system, do not add chlorox or any other chemicals to the water. Store your containers out of the sun light. Rotate the water once a year. When you go to use the water, it should be fine. But I intend to treat mine prior to use.

Now that you have information on how much water you require a day and ideas on to how store it, how much water does your family need?

Personally, I store a minimum two weeks supply for my family. When that runs out, I plan to use the water from the stream across the street.

You will have noticed that I intend to use the water from a contaminated stream. This water requires treatment before using it for drinking, cooking, dishwashing or brushing teeth. The following is a list of some of the more common and readily available methods for treating water.

First, if the water is muddy or turbid, let it set until the particles settle to the bottom, then drain the clear liquid off the top. You can also use a fine cloth or chamois to filter the water prior to treating it. A quick funnel can be manufactured by cutting the bottom out of a two-liter soda bottle. Turn it upside down and fill the neck with a fine weave clean cloth or chamois. Do not use the synthetic chamois that are now on the market. Fill the bottle with water through the bottom and let it filter through the cloth and out the neck of the bottle. This will not purify the water, but will take out the large partials and extend the life of your water filters.

Chlorine dioxide tablets manufactured by Aquamira, Micropur, and Portable Aqua, kill bacteria, viruses and cysts, including Giardia and Cryptosporidium. Chlorine dioxide is a well-established disinfectant. Chlorine dioxide is iodine and chlorine free. Chlorine dioxide tablets have a shelf life of four to five years depending on the brand. Check the expiration date on the package. Aquamira and Micropur meet the EPA guidelines for Microbiological Water Purifiers. The U.S. Military is currently switching from Iodine tablets to Chlorine Dioxide tablets.

Iodine tablets- One tablet added to a quart releases 8 ppm (parts per million) of iodine. Two tablets are used for turbid water. Wait 15 minutes after adding tablets, 30 minutes if the water is cold. The shelf life of the tablets is 3-5 years. Deterioration is evidenced by a change in the tablet color; metallic gray is acceptable, light yellow double the dose, and reddish brown discard. The formation of a precipitate is acceptable. If there is starch in the water from potatoes, corn or rice the water will turn a blue color. The blue colored water is harmless and is acceptable to drink. Iodine tablets are not effective against Giardia and Cryptosporidium. Iodine can have adverse health effects on some people.

Chlorox or chlorine bleach- Common household Chlorox or chlorine bleach may be used to disinfect water in the following amounts: Four drops per quart gives 10 ppm in clear water. This amount should be increased to eight drops in turbid water. Sixteen drops will provide 10 ppm per gallon of clear water. You should be able to get a slight odor of chlorox after the waters sits for the 15 minutes.

If not, add more chlorox. Chlorox or chlorinated bleach loses it strength with time. After one year on the shelf, it will have lost 50% of its strength, so double the dose. Remember to buy plain unscented bleach with no thickeners or additives.

Warning - Chlorine or iodine will not reliably kill Giardia and Cryptosporidium. At colder temperatures, doubling or tripling the wait time will improve your chances. SODIS, boiling, chlorine dioxide tablets and good water filters are more reliable.

Warning - Pregnant or nursing women or persons with thyroid problems should not drink water disinfected with Iodine.

Boiling - Bring the water to a rolling boil for at least three minutes. If you are over a mile above sea level, boil for at least five minutes.

Solar water disinfection (SODIS) - Pour clean water into Pet bottles and expose to sunlight for a minimum of six hours if the sky is bright or up to 50% cloudy. If the sky is 50 to 100 percent overcast, the container needs to be exposed to the sun for two consecutive days. Plastic bottles made from PET (PolyEthylene Terephtalate) or clear glass bottles are preferred. Avoid the use of bottles made of PVC (PollyVinylchloride). This method uses solar radiation and heat to destroy pathogenic microorganisms, which cause waterborne diseases. PVC bottles contain UV stabilizers, which blocks the sun's radiation.

PVC bottles often have a slight bluish color. When burned, PVC plastic gives off a pungent smelling smoke, the smell of burning PET is sweet. Heavily scratched or old bottles should be replaced due to a reduction of UV transmittance, which will reduce the efficiency of SODIS.

The following recycling table shows the image and unicode. One of these symbols is on the bottom of most bottles.

Recycling number	Image	Unicode	Abbreviation	Polymer name
1		#x2673;	PETE or PET	Polyethylene terephthalate
2		#x2674;	HDPE	High density polyethylene
3		#x2675;	PVC or V	Polyvinyl chloride
4		#x2676;	LDPE	Low density polyethylene
5		#x2677;	PP	Polypropylene

6		#x2678;	PS	Polystyrene
7		#x2679;	OTHER or O	Other plastics, including acrylic, acrylonitrile butadiene styrene, fiberglass, nylon, polycarbonat

Laying the bottles on sheets of corrugated sheet metal or on a roof will help speed the process. Attempts have been made to make large trays using window glass to purify water. Beware of this method; much of today's window glass has UV inhibitors or tints. The SODIS method was developed by the Swiss Federal Institute for Environmental Science and Technology and is recognized by the United States Center for Disease Control.

Backpack filters- There are many poor quality filters currently on the market. Make sure the filter you purchase will filter protozoa, bacteria and viruses down to 0.5 microns. Make sure your filter is certified to EPA Guide Standard for microbiological purifiers against bacteria, cysts and viruses. Three reputable brands are First Need, Katadyn and Aquamira. The Frontier Pro by Aquamira is currently my first choice. The filter is small, light, inexpensive and will purify about 50 gallons of water. Most backpack filters are limited in the quantity of water they will treat, often as little as 20 to 40 gallons. Check the specifications and buy the best you can afford, this is not the place to economize. Learn to use your filters. They take a little practice. Do not forget to store extra replacement filters.

Gravity flow filters - They are simple easy to use and can treat thousands of gallons of clean pre-filtered water. Merely pour the pre-filtered water in the top container and wait for it to flow though the filters into the bottom container. It requires no electricity, or special knowledge. The most recommended brands are the plastic American Berkefeld, the stainless steel British Berkefeld and the stainless steel Aqua Rain. Some of these filters can treat up to a gallon an hour. These units have been laboratory tested and will remove dangerous organisms such as protozoan cysts (Cryptosporidium, Giardia lamblia) and microscopic bacteria (E. coli, Salmonella typhimurium, etc).

For a permanent residence, a good gravity flow filter is superior and much more convenient. Gravity flow filters do not require chemicals. Since they operate by gravity, no pumping is required. They purify your water while you are free to do other things and they have a one to two gallon storage reservoir. A tap on the bottom reservoir is very convenient.

Aqua Rain gravity flow filter

American Berkefeld

Rainwater from your roof can be collected in a 55-gallon drum. Rig a downspout from your rain gutters to a clean barrel. Place a screen over the top of the barrel to prevent mosquitoes from breeding. Do not assume that the rainwater will be fit to drink without treatment. However when I was a child in South Africa, we drank untreated rainwater directly from the roof for a couple of years without ill effects. We did not attempt to treat it; the water was collected in a large galvanized tank with the faucet about 18 inches from the bottom. This allowed sediment to collect at the bottom of the tank. Remember, you have birds and insects living on the roof and their feces end up in the tank.

Chapter 3 - Food

The type of food that you store is a very personal matter. It depends on a combination of things: your normal diet, your budget and your storage space.

First, store food you and your family will consume. People always say that if they are hungry enough they will eat anything. Unfortunately, experience has shown this to be a fallacy. Additionally, a monotonous diet can rapidly become a problem particularly with the young.

How much food should you store? This depends on your goals. Why are you storing food and for how long do you think you will need it? My suggested plan consists of storing a three months supply of food that you will rotate through your normal diet. This will be backed up by enough long-term food for a year.

How do you accumulate this quantity of food without blowing your budget? First rule: do not go in debt. It is like the old joke: How do you eat an elephant? One bite at a time. Purchase something extra every month. Work at it steadily whenever you get a little extra cash.

Three Months Supply

The three months supply consists of canned food (wet pack), packaged foods and boxed cereals. In other words, the foods we eat in our normal diet, with a few exceptions, such as fresh and frozen foods. Items that require refrigeration can be included in this if you have a back up plan, such as salting or drying the food. If you live in a cold climate, you may be able to store food outdoors. A friend in Wyoming often stores meat in a small lean- to behind his house during the winter. Just remember to protect your cache from both two and four legged animals.

Canned food (also known as wet packed). A frequently asked question is how long is the shelf life of canned foods? Shelf life varies depending on the product. Foods having high acid content have the shortest shelf life. Tomato products are a good example.

A majority of cans have at least one or two dates on them: a best used-by date and a manufactured date that is often in code. The codes showing manufactured dates vary by manufacturer and usually include a time and place of canning. The best-used date is not an expiration date. Expiration dates can be determined by calling the toll free number that most manufacturers provide.

If correctly stored in moderate temperatures (below 70 degrees F), the majority of canned foods will last at least two years from the date of manufacture. Most canned products retain their safety and nutritional values long beyond these dates.

I have personally eaten canned goods that were over seven to eight years old. Prior to eating any out-of-date canned goods, check the cans carefully for bulges or leaks. When the can is opened, if it spits at you or shows a release of gas pressure, do not eat the foods. Try not to even touch the contents; there is a good chance that the can contains botulism. In theory, as long as the cans are sound and not bulging the food should be safe to eat. Canned foods 100 years old have been tested and found to be safe to eat, but I would not recommend it. Time always causes a loss of nutrition and a deterioration in taste. In my own storage, I have had to throw out cans that were bulged or leaking.

Rotate your short-term foods on a regular schedule. When you purchase canned products always check the use-by date to determine which products have the longest remaining shelf life. Do not buy dented or damaged cans. Beware of clearance houses and dollar stores; they often have products that are reaching the end of their shelf life.

Items that you may want to include:

Canned Products
Tuna
Any canned fish
Meats
Soup
Vegetables
Fruit
Condensed milk
Chili
Fruit or vegetable juice

Package Items
Spaghetti
Macaroni
Legumes (split peas, beans)
Instant potatoes
Soup mixes
Cake mixes
Pancake mix
Flour
Sugar
Honey
Crackers

Spices and Condiments
(There are some general rules for storing herbs and
spices. When possible, purchase whole spices.
Keep them cool and in dark places).
Salt
Pepper
Cayenne pepper
Bouillon cubes (beef and chicken)
Misc. spices
Ketchup
Mustard
Syrup
Jellies and jams

Oils and Fats
Olive
Canola
Corn oil
Canned shortening

Oil has a shelf life of one to two years before turning rancid. Canned Crisco shortening has the longest shelf life of any fats (except for freeze-dried butter). Some authorities claim that kept cool, its shelf life is almost indefinite. My recommendation is to be much more conservative and only store it for several years. With liquid oils, be sure to watch the expiration dates, and rotate them as needed. Extra virgin olive oil is reputed to have a slightly longer shelf life due because it is the first squeezing and therefore purer.

Rancid fats have been suspected of causing increases in arteriosclerosis, heart disease and cancer. When ever possible, keep oil away from light and oxygen and store in a refrigerator or cool place.

The above list is just a short list of suggested grocery items. Your list should be considerably longer. Remember to rotate your food.

Yeast - Active dry yeast should have a shelf life of approximately 1 year at 70 degrees. Keeping it refrigerated should extend the storage life to around 3 to 5 years. Freezing it will extend the storage life, but you should proof a sample every year to be sure it is still active. You proof yeast by mixing a small quantity of yeast with an equal amount of sugar. Add the mixture to warm water (105-115 degrees). Active yeast will begin to expand and become bubbly within five to ten minutes. If the reaction takes longer, you can still use the yeast, but you will need to use more. Yeast that shows no reaction should be discarded.

Vinegar is used for preserving food, as a condiment, salad dressing, medicinally, as a disinfectant and as a cleaner. There are numerous types of vinegars on the market, but for the purposes of this book we will only consider white distilled vinegar and apple cider vinegar. White distilled is not true vinegar but is actually diluted distilled acetic acid. It will store almost indefinitely if tightly sealed in a glass or plastic bottle with a plastic lid. The acid will destroy enamel-coated metal caps over time. It works well for pickling and most other uses.

Apple cider vinegar is sold in two types: one is a cider flavored distilled acetic acid, the other is a true cider vinegar fermented from hard cider. Fermented apple cider vinegar will occasionally form a cloudy substance. This is not harmful and can be filtered out prior to use. The cloudy substance is called Mother of Vinegar and can be used to make more vinegar. If the vinegar starts to smell bad, throw it away.

Long-Term Storage

Long-term storage foods are defined as foods that are considered safe and nutritious for extended periods, up to 30 years.

An example of long-term food items are freeze-dried, dehydrated and staple food items such as grains and beans with a low moisture content (10% or less) that can be stored for 20 to 30 years.

Oscar A. Pike, the lead researcher of BYU Long-term Food Storage Research team and chair of the Department of Nutrition, Dietetics and Food Science, answered the following questions about food storage:

Question: "How long will stored foods stay good?"

Answer: "There is a wide range in the shelf life of dried foods, depending on the specific commodity and its original quality, storage temperature, and so on. Some commodities should be used within a couple of years, like salad oil and dried eggs. However, many dried foods—packaged to remove oxygen and kept at room temperature or below—will store well for 20–30 years or more. In our studies, taste testers evaluated aroma, flavor, texture and overall acceptability of dried foods. Wheat and rice were very acceptable after 30-plus years of storage; beans, dried apples, macaroni, potato flakes, and oats up to 30 years; nonfat dry milk up to about 20 years."

Question: "Do foods that old retain their nutritional value?"

Answer: "There is a loss of nutrients over time, but there is sufficient nutritional value to justify storing dry foods long-term. In a survival situation, you need calories to stay alive, and stored foods provide calories. Vitamin C is another important nutrient and fortunately, vitamin C tablets retain a high percentage of their potency for more than 20 years."

How much should you store? Here are some guidelines on the amount of food you need for one adult for one year.

For an adult:

A combined 400 lbs of wheat, rice, other grains, beans and other legumes

60 lbs of sugar or honey

75 lbs of low fat powdered milk

5 lbs salt

If you intend to survive only on the above, it would provide enough calories, but barely meet nutritional standards. After a few days, the diet would become rapidly monotonous and the roughage would be hard on your system. If you supplement your diet with a garden and raise your own farm animals (chickens, cows, pigs, etc.), your nutritional needs will be taken care of. However, considering that the majority of us live in an urban environment, this is not practical. You need to store a mixture of dehydrated and freeze-dried foods to supplement your nutrition and provide variety.

Planning what you store may be one of the most important decisions that you are ever required to make. Too many people buy the food package provided by food storage dealers. They are often a one-size fits all package. Others work off a list provided by friends or obtained from books. The goal of this book is to teach you to think for yourself. You need a food package that fits your family, taking into consideration health problems and ages.

Let us discuss some common foods.

Wheat should be part of the 400 lbs of mixed grains and legumes that you store per person. Remember that about 40% of the population has a wheat allergy. Most allergies are mild and not of any consequence in our normal diet. If wheat were suddenly to become a large part of our diet, many individuals would have severe symptoms.

Personally, I store wheat; it is nutritious and has good protein value. The flour is versatile, and it is easy to crack for cereal. Sprouted wheat provides fresh greens high in vitamin C.

Hard red and hard white wheat are the best choices. They are the highest in gluten and protein, make excellent bread and store well. Kept in # 10 cans with oxygen absorbers, they should last for 30 years (see storage tips chapter 4).

White flour has approximately 1/3 the storage life of whole wheat.

Corn - When corn was first introduced into non-Native American farming, it was generally welcomed with enthusiasm for its productivity. However, a widespread problem of malnutrition soon arose wherever corn was introduced as a staple. This was a mystery since these types of malnutrition were not normally seen among the Native Americans to whom corn was the principal staple food.

It was eventually discovered that the Native Americans learned long ago to add alkali—in the form of wood ashes among North Americans and lime (calcium carbonate) among South and Central Americans—to corn meal. This liberates the B-vitamin niacin, the lack of which was the underlying cause of the condition known as pellagra.

Besides the lack of niacin, pellagra was also characterized by protein deficiency, the result of a lack of two key amino acids in corn, lysine and tryptophan. The Native Americans had learned to balance their consumption of corn with beans and other protein sources, such as meat and fish, in order to acquire the complete range of amino acids for normal protein synthesis.

Corn, despite its limitations, is still an excellent storage food. The best variety to store is yellow flint or dent corn. They are low moisture if properly dried. They make good polenta meal and flour. Popcorn should not be ground in most mills due to it extreme hardness. Several mills such as The Family Grain Mill and the Back T Basic Mill recommend that their mills not be used for popcorn.

Oats - Oats are mainly thought of as a bland breakfast food in the United States, but in Scotland and Ireland they were considered a staple. They are an excellent source of iron, dietary fiber and thiamin. One of the benefits of consuming oats is antioxidants, which are believed to protect the circulatory system from diseases such as arteriosclerosis, which affects the arterial blood vessels.

Uses of oats include cereals, a thickener for soups and stews, filler in meat loaf and casseroles, pancakes and baking. Regular and quick rolled oats are the most commonly stored and if properly packaged, can last 30 years.

Rice - It is probably the most consumed food in the world. White rice is the only form that is viable for long-term storage. If stored properly white rice will store almost indefinitely. Tests by Brigham Young University shows it to be edible and nutritious after 30 years of storage.

Rice is an excellent source of complex carbohydrates. All eight of the essential amino acids are contained in white rice. During the milling process, white rice looses approximately 10% of its protein, 70% of its minerals and 85% of its fat. In addition, thiamin, niacin and iron are lost during this process. Any rice sold as enriched has had thiamin, niacin and iron added after milling.

Brown rice is more nutritious, but due to its fat content should not be stored for any longer than 6 months, since it will turn rancid.

Legumes - This variety of food is one of highest in protein for non-animal foods containing between 20%-35%. It consists primarily of beans, peas and lentils. Legumes by themselves are not a complete protein, but when combined with other grains (wheat, rice) become a complete protein
.
Legumes include Beans of all types, a partial list includes
Black beans
Chickpeas or garbanzo beans
Kidney beans
Lima beans
Pinto beans
Soybeans
White beans

Long-term storage information on beans has not been readily available in the past. However, recent tests by Brigham Young University have established that black, white and pinto beans will store for over 30 years and still be acceptable for use. I have listed the reference for the test that I have been able to locate.

A study by C. M. LARSON, A. R. Sloan, L. V. Ogden, and O. A. Pike. Department of Nutrition,

Dietetics and Food Science, Brigham Young University, S-221 ESC, Provo, UT 84602 revealed the following:

"**Pinto beans** in restaurant-sized No. 10 cans are available in the retail market, but work is needed to determine the effects of long-term storage on quality. The objective of this research was to investigate the quality of retail-packaged pinto beans held at ambient temperatures up to 32 years."

"Twenty samples of pinto beans packaged in No. 10 cans and treated to remove oxygen were obtained from donors. Samples ranged from 1 to 32 years in age. Pinto bean samples were soaked in water containing varying levels of baking soda to standardize textural attributes. A 58-member consumer panel evaluated prepared pinto beans for appearance, aroma, texture, flavor and overall acceptability using a 9-point hedonic scale. Acceptance for use in everyday and emergency situations was also determined. Analyses included can headspace oxygen, can seam quality, color and water activity."

"Can headspace oxygen ranged from 2.1 to 20.7% respectively. All except two cans were hermetically sealed. Scores for flavor and overall acceptability, and the percentage of panelists who would eat pinto beans in everyday or emergency situations, decreased slightly with age. However, all samples that had been stored up to 30 years had greater than 80% acceptance for emergency use."

"Results indicate that though pinto beans experience a slight loss of quality during storage, they retain a high percentage of consumer acceptance over long periods of time and should be considered acceptable for use in long-term food storage efforts."

Various cultures worldwide have used a combination of grains and legumes for centuries as the staple of their diet. This has proved itself as the basis for a healthy diet.

All beans, even when they are correctly stored (see Chapter 4 Storage Tips), become harder over time and take more time to cook.

A method to help soften beans and speed up the cooking is as follows: First, sort and rinse the beans. Bring three cups of water to boil for each cup of beans. Add the beans to the boiling water and bring to a rolling boil for two minutes. Take the beans off the stove. Next, add 3/8 teaspoon of baking soda (sodium bicarbonate) for each cup of beans, cover and soak for 1 hour or more. Extra baking soda may be required for older beans. Drain and rinse the beans thoroughly. Cover the beans with water and bring to a boil, then reduce the heat and simmer 1-2 hours or until tender. Do not add salt or other ingredients until the beans have softened adequately.

Split peas - During the 16th and 17th centuries, split peas were used by the British Navy as a shipboard food with great success. Storage was in wooden casks, by today's standards, a very inadequate storage method.

Jordan S. Chapman, Brigham Young University, Provo, UT on a presentation made in July 30, 2007, stated the following: "Ten samples of split peas representing 5 retail brands packaged in size No.10 cans and stored at room temperature were obtained from donors. Two fresh samples of split peas were purchased as controls. Samples ranged in age from 1 to 34 years. Can headspace, oxygen, can seam integrity, and split pea water activity and color were evaluated. A 52-member consumer panel evaluated the samples, prepared as split pea soup, for appearance, aroma, texture, flavor and overall acceptability using a 9-point hedonic scale."

"Acceptance for use in everyday and emergency situations was also determined. Can headspace oxygen ranged from 0.19 to 20.1%. All can seams were determined to be satisfactory. Hedonic scores for texture declined over time, corresponding with increasing hardness of the peas. All samples had an acceptance in an emergency situation of over 75%. Results indicate split pea quality declines over time, but the product maintains sufficient sensory acceptance to be considered for use in applications requiring long-term storage."

When you purchase legumes or grains, the best choices are pre-cleaned products. Most obtained from food dealers will be pre-cleaned. If you are buying bulk from a producer or distributor, you may be buying field-run. This has not been cleaned and may be quite dirty. Know where your food comes from. Avoid animal feed products that may be subjected to fumigants that are forbidden for human consumption.

Nonfat dry milk - A strong source of calcium, protein and vitamin A. Regular nonfat dried milk is my personal choice for long-term storage. Its lack of fat keeps it from turning rancid. Tests at BYU indicate that properly stored in #10 cans with an oxygen absorber, it should last 20 years. The reason for recommending nonfat regular over instant milk is that it is more compressed, needs less storage space and is usually cheaper. The disadvantage is that it is a little harder to prepare.

If you purchase your milk in bulk, repack it into smaller containers. If left in the original bags its storage life will be greatly shortened and it will attract insects and rodents.

Tests conducted by the Department of Nutrition, Dietetics and Food Science, Brigham Young University, revealed the following information:

"Twenty samples of regular and instant nonfat dry milk (representing 9 brands) stored up to 29 years at ambient conditions were obtained from 14 sources. Samples were evaluated for headspace oxygen, can seam quality, water activity, solubility index, sensory quality (50-member consumer panel using a 9-point hedonic score), and nutritional value."

"Headspace oxygen ranged from 0.05%-20.9 percentage, which was related to the efficacy of the oxygen removal treatment (nitrogen, carbon dioxide or oxygen absorbers). Only six samples had less than 2% headspace oxygen. However, a 23-year old sample with low oxygen was not significantly different from fresh samples."

"Though there is some decline in quality over time, it appears possible to retain palatability and nutritional value in nonfat dry milk during long-term storage by using adequate packaging and storage conditions."

Baking powder Tests conducted by the Department of Nutrition, Dietetics and Food Science, Brigham Young University, revealed the following information:

"Baking powder is widely used to leaven baked products. The industry standard for baking powder shelf life is eighteen to twenty-four months, but little information is available on baking powder functionality when stored beyond this time."

"The objective of this research was to determine the effect of long-term storage on baking powder functionality. Six samples of double-acting baking powder in original commercial packaging were obtained from donors and two fresh samples were purchased. Samples ranged in age from 0.25-29 years and were stored in cool (15-25 °C) and dry conditions. Biscuits were made following standardized procedures and measured for height, diameter and surface crumb color."

"Under optimal storage conditions, it appears that baking powder retains its functionality as a leavening agent for many years and can be included in applications requiring long-term food storage."

Baking soda stored in its original containers and kept dry will store almost indefinitely.

Salt - I personally store an excessive amount of salt. It is cheap, stores indefinitely if protected from moisture and can be retained in its original packaging. Salt was used as a preservative prior to refrigeration (salt fish, salt pork, salt beef, etc.) Because of its many uses as a food preservative and its low cost, I store at least a 100 lbs of salt. Canning salt should be used as a preservative. This contains no additives such as iodide or anti-clumping agents. Canning salt may form clumps when exposed to moisture, but it does not hurt the salt. Just break up the clumps.

Sugar - Granular white and brown sugars have an indefinite storage life if stored in insect and moisture-proof containers.

Honey - Sweeter than sugar, it stores well. I prefer honey to sugar for personal use, although I store both. Honey has a tendency to crystallize with age. This is not a problem. In England when I was a child, it came this way from the store. I still like crystallized honey spread on bread. If you do not like it crystallized merely heat the container up in a large pan of hot water and it turns liquid.

Do not store honey in unlined metal containers. With age it takes on a metallic taste and turns black. You will not eat it.

Textured vegetable protein, or TVP, is a soy product, low in fat and high in fiber and protein. TVP is used by vegetarians and vegans to increase their protein intake and to mimic the texture of meat in a variety of dishes. Some emergency preparedness organizations recommend that people keep TVP, to have a readily available source of protein in a disaster.

TVP is made with defatted soy flour, which is a by-product of the manufacturing process used to make soybean oil. The soy flour is mixed with water, cooked, extruded and then dried. As it dries, the textured vegetable protein loses the bulk of its weight, turning into small flakes, which resemble breakfast cereal or perhaps dried vegetables.

TVP is a controversial subject. Many experts question the use of soybeans in our diet. There are strong indicators that they inhibit the body's digestion of some vitamins and proteins. Many flavored TVP products are reported to be high in sodium and MSG and some contain partially hydrogenated oils. I do not store it, preferring freeze-dried meats.

Additional low-moisture foods that store well over the long-term include macaroni, onion flakes, potato flakes (not pearls) and spaghetti.

Dehydrated and Freeze-Dried Foods.

One of the problems with long-term low-moisture foods is that many of them become deficient in vitamins A, C, B12 and calcium over time. The addition of dehydrated fruits and vegetables and freeze-dried meats can remedy this.

Vitamins A and C can be found in canned or bottled fruits and vegetables as well as in some fruit drink mixes. Most vitamin C is destroyed during dehydration of fruits and vegetables, but some vitamin A remains. Good sources of vitamin A include canned pumpkin and dehydrated carrots.

Vitamin B12 comes from animal products. It is found in canned meats, freeze-dried meats and jerky.

Calcium comes mainly from dairy products such as powdered milk, hot cocoa mix and pudding mix (containing dried milk).

Vitamin E is derived from fats and oils. Nuts such as sunflower seeds and almonds are a good source of vitamin E.

Dehydrated Food

Dehydrated foods consist primarily of fruits and vegetables that have had 98% of their moisture removed by drying. This process reduces the moisture in them to levels that inhibit the microbial growth that causes them to rot. They can be stored for extended periods if properly packed (Chapter 4 Storage Tips). Tests indicate that they retain their nutritional value and taste. Dehydration also reduces weight, which makes them a great backpacking and survival food. I have listed some examples below.

Dehydrated carrots - An excellent source of vitamin A. Tests presented by Stephanie R. Bartholomew, Brigham Young University showed the following:

"Dehydrated carrots packaged in hermetically sealed cans with a reduced oxygen atmosphere are available in the retail market. To determine the effects of long-term storage, eleven samples of dehydrated carrots representing 6 brands, packaged in size No.10 cans and stored at room temperature, were obtained from donors. Two fresh samples were purchased as controls. Samples ranged in age from less than 1 to 34 years. Can headspace oxygen can seam integrity, and dehydrated carrot water activity and color were evaluated. Samples were hydrated for 20 minutes in filtered water that was brought to a boil. A 56-member consumer panel evaluated the dehydrated carrots for appearance, aroma, texture, flavor and overall acceptability using a 9-point hedonic scale. Acceptance for use in everyday and emergency situations was also determined."

"All samples had an acceptance for use in an emergency situation of over 70%. Results indicate that dehydrated carrots decline in quality during long-term storage but retain sufficient sensory acceptance to be considered for use in long-term storage regimens."

"Test indicated that carrots packed in #10 cans with an oxygen absorber and properly stored would last for 25 years."

I have mentioned carrots in such detail because it is a product that has undergone extensive testing. Many other foods such as the following, peas, corn, onions, apples, etc., store long-term if properly packed.

Understand that dehydration is merely removing the moisture, or old-fashioned drying. You can do it at home with a food dehydrator or even in your backyard using the sun.

I have a friend who buys frozen mixed vegetables, green beans, peas or corn when on sales. He dries them in an electric food dehydrator making sure that they are completely dried. Without doing anything to them other than placing them in a zip lock plastic bag, he has successfully kept them for over five years and they were still edible. The nutritional contents have not been tested. I would recommend canning them with an oxygen absorber if you intend to place them in long-term storage. This will help preserve nutrition.

Freeze-Drying

Freeze-drying is the process of drying foods by placing frozen foods in a vacuum at absolute pressures that permits ice to change directly to vapor. In other words, this can be compared to freezer burn, but is so fast that the food shows no effect.

The type of products typically freeze-dried includes meats, fishes, shrimp, instant coffee, vegetables and fruits.

Advantages
Little thermal damage
Excellent flavors
Good vitamin retention
Rehydrates rapidly
Little shrinkage
Long product storage life 25 years—if suitably packed

Disadvantages
High production costs
Not good for everything
Rapid deterioration unless products are packaged and stored properly
Cannot be done at home

Warning -If you intend to store meat, cheeses or similar products, it is strongly recommend that you choose freeze-dried. When you purchase freeze-dried or dehydrated products, ask about the residual oxygen. This is the amount of oxygen left in the can when it is ready for sale. There are numerous inferior products on the market. Anything you buy should be in good quality metal cans and have no more than 5% residual oxygen and preferable no more than 2%. If your supplier cannot provide you with this information and back it up with laboratory tests, run!

Chapter 4 - Storage Tips

The first rule of food storage can be summed up in the acronym HALT. It stands for the four enemies of good food storage. These are Humidity, Air (oxygen), Light and Temperature. This is the basis of all food storage.

The following are some facts you need to understand:

Plastic food grade containers - This includes all sizes of plastic buckets. Containers of food grade quality are manufactured from polycarbonate, polyester or polyethylene. All sizes vary in characteristics in terms of density, permeability and strength. Only buckets manufactured from food grade plastics and having a gasket in the lid seals should be used to store food.

An important fact to understand is that most plastic is permeable; in other words, it breathes. Unless lined with Mylar bags you cannot count on plastic buckets to protect food from oxygen. Do not store food in plastic bags or buckets near gasoline, kerosene or other chemicals - they may pickup the taste and odor.

Typically, wheat and beans have been stored in plastic buckets without Mylar bags. Based on the observation of others and myself, I feel this method works. I have used wheat stored this way that is 20 years old. Today based, on recent tests, wheat, and beans stored only in plastic buckets, while edible are probably not as nutritious as those stored in Mylar bags or metal cans and protected from oxygen. All my new grains and legumes are now stored in #10 cans with oxygen absorbers.

Warning: Do not stack plastic buckets over three high. With age many buckets become brittle and collapse if stacked too high. If the buckets are stacked, periodically check the buckets to ensure that the lids have not broken from the weight.

Food grade Mylar bags. Mylar bags create an oxygen barrier to protect food during extended long-term storage. Mylar bags can be clear or metalized. Mylar bags are used by some of the better food companies to line their plastic buckets to create an oxygen barrier.

Metalized Mylar bags can be used independently for food storage. They can be sealed with either a standard bag sealer or a common household iron. Just be sure to tug on the seal to make sure it is tight. Mylar bags come in varying sizes and thickness. The most common is 4 millimeters.

Aluminum coated plastic pouches are frequently mistaken for Mylar bags. They possess similar characteristics and are frequently used interchangeably with Mylar bags. Seal them only with an approved pouch sealer. Irons will not provide an adequate seal, especially for powdered products such as flour or dry milk.

Advantages of Mylar bags and aluminum coated plastic pouches.
Can hold a vacuum
Inexpensive
Lightweight
Requires little special equipment to use
Can be reused

Disadvantages
They are not rodent proof
Odd shaped, awkward to store
They are subject to being easily torn

Metal cans - Cans are available in several sizes, the most common being Numbers 10, 2-1/2 and 303. These numbers indicate the standard sizes for each can. A #10 can generally holds 13 cups. The #303 can holds 2 cups and the #2-1/2 container holds 3-1/2 cups - just 1/2 cup shy of a quart. A # 10 can is 5/6 of a gallon. If you have access to a can sealer and oxygen absorbers, cans are the best method of storing dry products for long-term storage in my opinion.

Advantages
Rodent proof
Waterproof
Can hold a vacuum
Easy to move and store

Disadvantages
Cannot be resealed
More expensive than Mylar bags
Subject to rust

Glass bottles - For many years glass bottles have
been use to store dried foods successfully. Oxygen
absorbers work well in glass bottles because glass is
an excellent vapor barrier. Make sure that glass
bottles are protected from breakage in case of an
earthquake or other disaster.

Oxygen absorbers - Placed in a non-permeable
container they absorb the available oxygen.
Oxygen is the main cause of food spoilage. It
allows pests and molds to grow in your food.
Eliminating oxygen in your long-term food storage
containers ensures the longest possible shelf life.

Oxygen absorbers work with a simple chemical
process. They contain iron powder and salt, which
reacts with the oxygen in the air causing the iron
powder to rust. When all the iron powder has
rusted, the oxygen absorbers are finished and the
absorbing action stops.

The reason that the container needs to be non-
permeable is that when the oxygen is absorbed, the
container maintains a partial vacuum. The number
of oxygen absorbers required depends on the size of
the container. A 500 CC oxygen absorber is more
than adequate for a # 10 can. For a five or six
gallon container, you should use three 500 CC

oxygen absorbers. Remember, if you are using plastic buckets and oxygen absorbers, the buckets need to be lined with a non-permeable barrier such as Mylar.

There are two common types of oxygen absorbers on the market. One is beige and turns a blue- green when expended. The second is bright pink and turn too a dark blue green when expended. When you use oxygen absorbers remember, always read the instructions that come with them. Do not eat the contents of the oxygen absorber packets.

If you are purchasing your food products already packed, look for the following:

Any grains or legumes sold in plastic buckets should have Mylar liners.

Freeze-dried products should have the oxygen removed by one of the following methods.
Vacuum packed
Nitrogen filled (preferred method)
Oxygen absorber

The residual oxygen should be no more than 5%, preferably less than 2%. Again, I repeat, if your supplier cannot provide you with this information and back it up with lab tests. Run and find another dealer.

A reputable supplier will not have any problem providing you with information about the residual oxygen. One supplier that I have dealt with for many years describes his packaging in the following manner: "The cans are nitrogen packed replacing air with nitrogen. Each can is coated with protective enamel, including the lid. This enamel helps protect the can from the deteriorating elements of oxygen and moisture. The contents of the can are protected for many years. Our foods will have the longest shelf life available...in excess of 30 years! As long as the can is not opened or punctured." He has lab reports documenting that his products contain less than 2% oxygen. See Freeze Dry Guy in the list of references at end of book.

Many people have access to can and Mylar bag sealers. There is nothing wrong with packaging your own products. There are a few things to be careful of.

Since you are probably using oxygen absorbers, you have to realize that they start to work as soon as they are exposed to air. Open and shut the bags as rapidly as possible. When you purchase your oxygen absorbers, ask about the bag clips that are available to help keep the oxygen absorbers fresh.

Check the seals on both the cans and the Mylar bags. The can seals should be flat and tight; Mylar bag seals should be continuous and not pull apart when subject to light stretching.

Remember to date your cans and mark what is in them. I know people who have a pile of unmarked mystery cans in their storage. When you open your cans, use a resealable plastic lid to protect the contents from moisture. The products are best if used within a month or two after opening.

At the beginning of the chapter the acronym, HALT was mentioned. If you follow the proceeding packaging methods, you have taken care of the air, light, an oxygen portions.

The ideal storage area is a dry spacious basement that maintains a temperature of 70 degrees or less all year round. If you are lucky enough to have these conditions all you have to do is arrange your shelves so that the products have air space between the floor and exterior walls.

As for most of us, we have to cram food into all the nooks and crannies of our homes. Normally garages are too hot in the summer to make good storage areas. If possible, you want a storage area where the temperatures do not exceed 70 degrees.

I cannot give you a simple answer on how to store your food. A wise man once said that if you have to use your storage, you would wish you had kept the furniture in the garage and the food in the house!

You have to use your imagination. I have seen bookcases made with five-gallon buckets and box springs set on number 10 cans. Many newer homes have pantries. If your home has a wood floor with a crawl space underneath, you can use an old trick to help cool your pantry. Install a vent in the floor and one in your attic to create an upward airflow from the cool crawl space. Under floor crawl spaces can make excellent storage areas if you do not have a moisture problem.

Old Fashion Storage Methods

Canning- not really old fashioned, but not as common as it once was. I am not going to tell you how to can, but in the References section you will find some useful resources. Just remember when you store glass jars to protect them from breakage.

How to keep food cool - without ice or refrigeration. An iceless refrigerator that uses water for cooling is still in use in many third world countries. It is simple and cheap to build. The instructions for constructing one are in Chapter 9.

Drying

An old friend of mine still remembers the method they used when he was a child in the South as follows:

Green beans were strung by using a needle and strong thread. Tie a knot in one end and push the needle through the center of the beans, pushing the beans towards the knot. When you get 2 or 3 feet of beans on the string, hang the beans up by the end in a warm dry area, but out of direct sunlight. Let them hang until the beans are dry. Store in a paper or cloth bag until ready for use.

Peas, when the peas are ripe, lay them in the sun to dry. After they are dry, wait for a windy day. Place them on a sheet and beat the hulls off with a stick. The wind will blow the chaff away and leave just the peas. Store the peas in a paper or cloth bag until use.

Corn, cut the corn off the cob and lay in the sun until dry.

My friend says most vegetables can be dried without any special instructions if you just use your common sense. Use good sanitation practices. Do not attempt to dry vegetables, which are badly bruised or have any rot. Keep the vegetables clean and protect them from insects during the drying process. Window screens can be used to make a box allowing airflow but protecting the vegetables from flies, etc. Check the Reference Section for information on drying food and other methods such as pickling.

Another method of drying is to use your car. If you do not have gasoline to drive your car, you can use the car as a drier. Place your drying racks across the backs of the seats and just leave the windows slightly cracked. Sitting in the sun with the window just cracked, the car gets very hot. This speeds up your drying process and gives you some protection against insects and dirt.

Brining

Brining is commonly used for the preservation of meat and fish. The basic process of brining is to add approximately 8 lbs of salt to 5 gallons of water. A method of determining the correct concentration is with a raw egg. The ideal brine has enough salt to float a raw egg. You will need enough brine to submerge the meat or produce without any portion being exposed to air. Some meat products might require being weighed down to stay submerged. Leave the food in the brine until ready to consume. Use canning salt for brining. This has no additives. Most stores stock canning salt in their canning supply section. Using salt with additives or impurities can produce less than desirable results, especially with fish. Fish must be cleaned prior to brining.

Any food grade HDPE, PP or polycarbonate container is appropriate for brining. These materials can withstand the salt in brines. These containers will normally have the recycling number two (see chart in Water Storage Chapter 2).

As a general rule: Food storage containers sold at restaurant supply stores are made of food grade HDPE, PP or polycarbonate. The interior of ice chests and freezers are made of food grade HDPE. Any white, opaque plastic bucket that contains food for human consumption is made of food grade HDPE.

Manage your Food Supply.

Keep track of the dates of your perishable foods such as wet pack, and rotate them often to insure having the freshest product when you need it.

Date your cans or cases. Use a marking pen and write on the cans.

Watch for rodent or insect infestation in bulk packed items.

Check for rancidity. When in doubt, open and inspect. I would rather open a few items unnecessarily than find that they had gone bad when I needed them most.

If you don't want the hassle of managing your food storage (most people, including me, are too lazy), then buy the best quality freeze-dried and dehydrated foods and grains in #10 or #2-1/2 size cans from someone you trust.

Maintain an inventory of your long-term food storage.

Chapter 5 - Cooking, Lights and fuel

The premise of this chapter is that the electric grid is nonfunctioning or unreliable for an extended period. You are dependent on your own resources.

Generators are handy for short-term power outages. It is not possible for most of us to store enough gasoline to make generators practical for long-term use. A good quality generator can cost upward of a thousand dollars. Unless you have the capability to store several hundred gallons of gasoline, I do not recommend that you invest your money in a generator. This money can purchase a lot of food and other supplies.

Warning: Cooking, heating and lighting units (this includes gasoline motors) that burn fuel of any type give off gases. Most unvented appliances should not be used in a closed area because they give off carbon monoxide. Carbon monoxide will kill you if not properly vented.

Alcohol burns clean and gives off almost no products of combustion. Kerosene gives off carbon dioxide, which is less dangerous than carbon monoxide. Alcohol and kerosene are the safest of the fuels to burn in unvented appliances. Alcohol and kerosene lamps can be used in your home.

None of these appliances should be left on overnight or while sleeping. Do not under any circumstance burn charcoal in an enclosed area as it gives off carbon monoxide and will kill you.

Carbon monoxide is not toxic in the normal sense. It combines with the hemoglobin in your blood and starves the cells of needed oxygen, which results in internal suffocation. Breathing a concentration of 1000 parts per million will kill you in a relatively short period of time. Carbon monoxide is a colorless, odorless gas.

The symptoms of carbon monoxide poisoning can include headache, dizziness and confusion, pink to reddish skin color, nausea, vomiting and fainting. The only treatment is to give victims oxygen or exposure to fresh air.

I am sure some of you remember your grandparents violating some of these rules in past years. You also need to remember, that their houses were often drafty and not well insulated.

Matches - Everybody likes to think that they are Daniel Boone and that it is easy to start a fire with one match. It is just not that easy. Go out in your yard, try it, and when you think you are good at it, try it with wet wood. Matches are cheap; you can buy a lot for a few dollars. Store more than you think you will ever need. If nothing else, they will be good trading stock

Solar is one possible solution. If you are dedicated enough and willing to spend the money you can go completely off the grid. I am not going to attempt to recreate the wheel by telling you how to put in a full solar system. Refer to the Reference Section.

Solar ovens are one of my favorite solutions to the problems of cooking. In most areas of the United States, you can cook with a solar oven for most of the year. A friend in Wyoming has boiled water in his with the oven sitting on four feet of snow. You can bake bread, cook stews and boil water - just about anything, but frying in a solar oven. A common question asked about solar ovens is, will they brown food when you bake? The answer is yes.

Solar cooking is clean, keeps the heat outside, and the food tastes good. Obtain your solar oven and practice with it now. In an emergency, you do not want to waste food experimenting with it. A general rule for solar cooking is that it takes about twice the normal amount of cooking time. If you cut your food into smaller pieces, it will cook faster.

Once you put your food in the oven, try not to open the lid any more than necessary. Your temperature can drop up to 100 degrees every time you open the lid. Do not use stainless steel or bright aluminum cookware - it will reflect the heat instead of holding it.

Quart glass jars painted black work well for cooking pots. Prior to painting a jar, run a piece of one-inch tape from top to bottom on one side. After painting, remove the tape. This will give you a window, so you can check on your food during cooking. Cast iron is great on partially cloudy days because it retains heat and keeps cooking temperatures even.

Other uses for your solar oven include pasteurizing water, killing insect infestations in grains or dried foods, drying firewood or tinder and heating water for dishwashing or sanitation.

Many sites on the internet sell solar ovens in the $100 to 300 dollar range. Solar ovens are easy to improvise and can be made for under $30. A simple solar oven plan is in Chapter 9; and there are references to some excellent websites in the Reference Section.

Both of these solar ovens work well. The one on the right is made of two cardboard boxes, one inside the other with newspapers shoved between them for insulation and lined with an old windshield sun reflector. The top is two pieces of tempered glass a neighbor gave me. The one on the left is a metal box lined with silver colored Styrofoam insulation. The lid is lined with aluminum foil. A piece of 1/8 inch Plexiglas is used for the top.

Wood stoves are a great way to go: they can provide heat as well as cooking. In some areas of the country, the government is attempting to ban them or limit the days you may use them for generating pollution. Depending on the type of stove and the climate you live in, you may need from one to five cords of wood per winter.

However, they come with some built-in problems. First, make sure that they are correctly installed and vented. If not correctly installed, they can become a fire hazard. Follow the manufacture's instructions and local building code recommendations for clearances from combustible materials.

If you intend to depend on a wood stove, make sure that you stock the necessary implements for cutting and splitting firewood. This includes axes, splitting malls and an old-fashioned crosscut saw. Do not forget the files to sharpen them.

Rocket stoves - A simple homemade stove that can be made from old tin cans and scrap metal. This type of stove is extremely efficient; it will generate an amazing amount of heat burning small twigs and sagebrush. If you were faced with a shortage of fuel, this would be a great stove to own. It will burn the twigs, dried brush and other small debris that most people ignore.

The stove shown below which is made from a five-gallon can and some scrap 4-inch pipe, works well. A plan for manufacturing one is in Chapter 9.

Rocket Stove

Camping stoves - In this class, I am including Coleman style camp stoves and others that run on white gas (Coleman Fuel), propane or butane with the exception of the small backpack stoves.

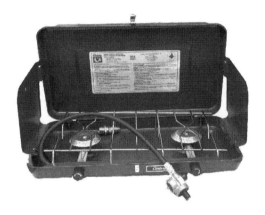

Coleman Propane Stove

The older Coleman stoves are a good product and are quite efficient. The problem with them is the type and quantity of fuel you have to store. White gas and Coleman fuel are highly flammable; storing any quantity is dangerous without adequate safeguards and in many areas are a violation of fire codes.

Many of the new Coleman-style stoves run on small non-refillable propane tanks. Conversion kits are available so that these can be connected to larger five-gallon propane tanks. This let you cook for longer periods of time and reduces your costs. Propane is much safer to store than white gas.

If your home runs on propane, you may have several hundred gallons available in the tank in your yard. When the power fails, most modern propane appliances will not run without electricity. Make sure you have the necessary plumbing supplies on hand to connect your stove to your propane line. Any good hardware store should be able to supply the needed parts.

If you go to one of the better camping/backpacking stores, you will find a selection of excellent small backpacking stoves. Most of these are so small, they are not practical for everyday use. They belong in your 72-hour kit. I would not depend on them for my main cook stove. They utilize bottled butane, propane, wood and flammable liquids for fuel. My personnel choice would be one that uses wood or flammable liquid. You have a better chance of finding replacement fuel in an emergency. They are light, easy to use, and quite practical for a few day's use.

Kerosene stoves are commonly used in many third world, African and Asian countries. The brand that I am familiar with is the Butterfly stove from Malaysia. It is inexpensive, reliable and available. There are several sources on the Internet. In the Reference Section, I have listed one that I have dealt with and found reliable. The Butterfly stove is

available in one and three burner models. The
single burner model will run for approximately 12
hours on a gallon of fuel. The wicks are easily
changed and are good for up to six months.

While the storage of fuel is always a bit of a
problem, I feel these stoves are very worthwhile.
Twenty gallons of kerosene would provide you with
approximately 240 hours of cooking. Depending on
your climate, if you share the cooking with a solar
oven on sunny days, you could cook for a year with
a relatively small amount of kerosene (20 gallons).

Butterfly oven

Butterfly also manufactures an oven that works as a
companion to the Butterfly stoves. It is capable of
baking bread. The oven is designed so that it sits on
top of the stove. It can also be set on a grill over
hot coals

Single-burner Butterfly stove The glass bottle holds the kerosene and feeds the stove by gravity.

Sixteen wick

Butterfly stoves has recently come out with a new version known as the 16 wick stove. This stove produces more heat than previous models and works better with the oven for baking bread. The downside to this stove is that it uses about twenty-five percent more fuel.

In an emergency, a Butterfly stove can serve as a heater. Place a brick, large rock or a piece of heavy metal on the burner, and turn the heat up. The mass will work as a heat sink and help disperse the heat evenly. This will not be as efficient as a kerosene heater, but it will warm a small room.

When first lit, all kerosene stoves will smoke a little since the burners do not provide maximum efficiency until it they are warm. Cracking a few windows will solve the problem. When you are through using a kerosene stove, do not blow it out. Turn down the wick and let it burn out. This will use up the kerosene vapors remaining in the wicks, and help eliminate kerosene odors.

Butane stoves

There are small one-burner butane stoves being sold in many retail stores. My experience with the stoves is that they work well. The downside is that the fuel comes in aerosol cans. It you intend to utilize one of these stoves for any period of time, you will need to store a large number of fuel cans. While the stoves are inexpensive, the cost of the fuel canister mounts up quickly.

Butane Camp Stove

How to Cook Your Food Over an Open Campfire.

If you are like most of the population of the United States, you have not lit a campfire in many years. Lighting campfires takes practice and experience. In an emergency, matches will be in short supply. Learn how to start a fire now. I have seen inexperienced people use whole boxes of kitchen matches and still not have a fire started. Learning to light fires cannot be stressed strongly enough. If you cannot start a fire in the rain with wet wood, you have not practiced enough.

The pioneers used tripods to hang their cooking pots over open fires. These are easy to duplicate with ½-inch rebar and a short length of chain. These items are available at any building supply. Remember to be fire safe.

A typical layout of a pioneer campfire. Notice the chain to hang pots from, it is doing double duty by holding one end of the spit

Dutch ovens - These were widely used by the pioneers due to their versatility. Dutch oven cooking is an art all by itself. Before purchasing a Dutch oven, consider the following

- Buy only Dutch ovens with legs. There should be three legs, firmly attached.

- The lid should fit tight with no gaps around the rim and have a lip around the top to hold hot coals.

- The casting and thickness of the metal should be even, especially around the rim. Large variations will create hot and cold spots during cooking.

- Make sure the lid has a loop handle tightly attached to its center.

- The bail or wire handle should be attached firmly to the pot. The bail should be easily movable and strong enough to carry or support a heavy pot full of stew.

Dutch ovens can be used over an open fire. They also work well in a solar oven or with practically any other type of stove. They can be hung over an open fire or placed in the hot coals. You can then scoop up hot coals and place them on the lid. This gives you even heat on the top and bottom, which permits you to bake bread, rolls and even cake.

Many of the Dutch Ovens that you currently see on the market are aluminum. I would recommend that you avoid them and stay with cast iron. Aluminum is lighter in weight, but has a tendency to cool rapidly. With aluminum, it is much harder to keep

74

an even heat while cooking. This makes it harder to bake.

A typical dutch oven camp kitchen. Notice the hot coals on top of the Dutch ovens. This provides an even heat. The spit can be used to roast meat.

Many new cast iron frying pans and Dutch ovens come from the manufacturer with a waxy coating. This needs to be burned off prior to use. The best way is to turn the oven upside down over an open fire or charcoal. When they heat up, you will see the waxy coating bubble up. Let this burn out and wipe with a clean rag. You are now ready to season your pot.

To season a cast iron pot, coat the pot with lard, bacon grease or Crisco and bake at 250 degrees for 4 hours. Do not use a liquid vegetable oil or the pan will be sticky and not properly seasoned.

After cooking, wash the pan while still warm in hot water and scrape the pan if needed. Do not use scouring pads or soap; they will break down the pan's seasoning. If your pan rusts, it needs to be re-seasoned.

Lighting

Candles - While this is one of the oldest methods of lighting, it is not necessarily the best method. Even good quality wax candles give off significantly less light than a kerosene lantern.

The biggest advantage of candles is that if you shop carefully, you can purchase them quite inexpensively. After Christmas and other holidays, you often see them on sale. You can buy a few every month and gradually build up your stock. Some of the 100-hour candles sold by survival supply stores contain liquid paraffin fuel and are not a true candle. The flame they provide is a little brighter.

Remember, with all candles you are dealing with an open flame and they are a fire hazard. Stock some good candleholders. You can stick one or more candles into a plant pot filled with dirt and place a piece of shiny metal or a mirror behind it for an improvised candleholder.

Butane and propane lanterns - These are good reliable products. Most provide plenty of light, and use fuel efficiently. Some of the propane models can be converted to work with 5 gallon or larger propane tanks. If you intend to use this type of lighting, remember to purchase at least a dozen extra mantles and any fittings you need to convert to larger propane tanks. Read the instructions that come with them. Butane lanterns cannot be converted to propane. Avoid cheap foreign manufactured knock-offs.

Solar lighting -A friend of mine has created a simple 12-volt solar system for a few hundred dollars. He mounted two small solar panels on the south side of his home. He uses them to keep a pair of 12-volt deep cycle marine batteries charged. This provides power to several 12-volt lights located throughout his residence. Check the Reference Section under solar.

Flashlights - A good flashlight can save your life. You need them in your home, car and 72-hour kit. With the advent of the LCD bulb, flashlights have become smaller and more efficient. Always keep your flashlights in the same spot so during an emergency you can find them in the dark.

There are currently numerous flashlights on the market that do not require batteries. They operate by shaking, squeezing or cranking. Before you buy any of these, check to see where they are manufactured. Many of the ones on the market are of poor quality and could not be relied on in an emergency. I have not found any of the flashlights that function by shaking to meet my requirements. The only thing I can say about them is that they are better than nothing.

LCD bulbs have extremely long lives, but it is not practical to replace bulbs in these flashlights when they go bad. Good quality non-LCD flashlights like Maglights have spare bulbs stored inside the base. If your flashlight uses incandescent bulbs, be sure to store extra bulbs.

Extra batteries should be kept refrigerated or as cool as possible. This prolongs their shelf life. There are currently small solar chargers on the market that will work with rechargeable batteries. Many of the larger chain electronic stores carry them. I would recommend getting a solar charger and rechargeable batteries as well as a good stock of standard batteries. If possible, standardize the size of batteries and type of flashlight you use. You can always cannibalize one to repair another.

Kerosene lanterns were in common use prior to the advent of electricity. They provide good light and are efficient and simple to use. You can purchase hurricane lamps quite inexpensively for under $10.

Kerosene lanterns provide approximately 68 lumens of light or about 6 candlepower. Older Petromax kerosene lanterns provide 1300 lumens of light. They are much more efficient than a hurricane lamp. The table below compares the fuel use to the amount of light given. You can see that a Petromax lantern is comparable to a 100-watt light bulb. The downside to the Petromax is that they are more expensive, costing in the area of $130.00. If you decide to obtain a Petromax, be sure to get a real one, not one of the cheap copies made in Asia.

Fuel consumption

Light source (fuel)	Light output lumens (lm)	Fuel consumption	Efficacy (lm/W)
100 W bulb (electricity)	1340	100 W	13.4
Hurricane (kerosene)	68	16 g/hr	0.35
Petromax (kerosene)	1300	80-90 g/hr	1.27
Fluorescent tube, 40 W (electricity)	2400	40 W	60.00

Information in this table is from the Nimbkar Agricultural Research Institute (NARI), Phaltan-415523, Maharashtra (India).

BriteLyt lanterns are a new product manufactured by Petromax. They claim to run on a variety of fuels. Kerosene, alcohol-based fuels (with adapter), mineral spirits, citronella oil, gasoline, Biodiesel, diesel fuel, Coleman fuel, JP fuels, & almost every flammable fuel available on the market. The company is currently manufacturing them for the U.S. Military. They have two different size lanterns, the CCP 150 & CCP 500. The CCP 500 can be fitted with attachments for heating and cooking.

The CCP 150 can provide a light equal to a 300-watt bulb and the CCP 500 equal to a 550-watt bulb. They have a reputation for having a bit of a learning curve and come with an instructional DVD. Watch the DVD and practice lighting your BriteLyt while times are good.

From left to right: battery operated LCD lantern, BriteLyt CCP 150, Propane lantern, Coleman Lantern, Hurricane Lantern, Kerosene Lantern

Chapter 6 - Medical and Sanitation

Emergency Medical Supplies

The following list was prepared with the advice of a doctor, but like the term first aid implies, this list is limited in its application. The quantities of first aid supplies required for your family will depend on it's size. This is not a complete list; contact your own medical provider for advice on any of your special medical needs.

Abdominal pad 5" x 9", minimum of 6
Absorbent gauze pads 2x2, 4x4
Adhesive tape (1/2", 1" and 2")
Airway, pharyngeal, plastic, adult, and child sizes
Antiseptic, such as Betadine
Assorted Band-aids
Bandage roller, assorted sizes
Blade, surgical knife, sizes 10, 11 and 15, one-half
  dozen each
Blood stopper kit
Burnfree Dressings
Butterfly bandages
Cotton, absorbent, sterile
Cotton tipped swabs
CPR mask
Ear syringe
Elastic bandage 3", minimum 2
Eye pads
Forceps, 6" assorted, both straight and curved
Handle, scalpel #3, for detachable surgical knife
  blades

Gloves, disposable vinyl, nitrile or latex gloves,
  minimum of one box
Multi Trauma dressing, 12" x 30"
Petroleum jelly
First aid book
Roller gauze 1" and 2"
Respirators N-95, minimum level of respiratory
  protection is a surgical mask or preferably an N95
  respirator
Safety pins
Scissors, bandage and straight
Sphygmomanometer, aneroid (blood pressure cuff)
Splints two 36" SAM Splints plus two 4" rolls of
  cohesive Wrap
Sponges 4" X 4" Sterile, minimum 10
Stethoscope
Surgical soap
Sutures, assorted
Suture holder
Thermometer, old style mercury thermometers, both
oral and rectal
Tongue depressors
Tourniquet
Triangular bandage 40" x 40" x 56"
Tweezers

Non-prescription medication

Alcohol, rubbing
Antacid
Anti-diarrhea medication
Aspirin, Tylenol or Excedrin

Baking soda
Calamine lotion
Eyewash
Gatorade powder, used for dehydration
Hydrocortisone ointment
Hydrogen peroxide
First Aid cream
Laxative such as Senekot
Multi-vitamin and vitamin C
Salt
Sunscreen

Store your required prescription medications as needed. Freezing will extend the shelf life of some medications. Consult your own doctor or pharmacist.

The above list of medical supplies is only as good as the person utilizing them. Take an advanced first aid class, learn CPR or consider becoming an EMT. There are some good medical books listed in the Reference Section.

Sanitation

This is a subject not to be taken lightly. During all the wars the United States fought prior to World War 2, more men died of disease than combat. At times, diseases caused two deaths for every one killed in combat. This was a result of bad water and unsanitary conditions. Water has been addressed in Chapter 2; other sanitary issues will now be discussed.

Disease and human waste -Today we are lucky to live in a world of flush toilets and plenty of toilet paper. Tomorrow we may have to live like our ancestors. The disposal of human waste has been a major cause of disease for most of human history. The exception has been the last 100 years.

I have known friends who have large food storages, but have not considered hygiene. Your need for sanitation supplies will vary depending on the number of individuals using your facilities and your location.

Items That I recommend Storing are:

Hand soaps - Bar soap keeps better than the new liquids, which can evaporate, if stored in the heat. Figure out how much hand soap you use in a given period and double the amount. You will probably be dirtier than normal.

Dish soap, liquid or powder. The soap should be biodegradable because you may have to use the grey water for your garden. Look for soaps that will work well in cold water.

Laundry soap - It should be biodegradable; you may have to use the grey water for your garden. Consider putting in a clothesline. Do you have a washboard and tub? Some of the suppliers listed in the Reference Section have hand wringers and other alternatives to washboards, etc.

Disinfectants such as Pinesol, Lysol and Hexol, are good to have on hand in case of illness. Bleach is a good disinfectant; it is inexpensive and purifies water. Nevertheless, remember, it needs to be rotated. It looses half its strength in one year.

Feminine supplies - How much you stock depends on your family's needs, but be generous. The individually wrapped feminine napkins make good first aids dressings. In the past, women have used rags and pads of moss.

Diapers - Be old fashioned and stock cloth diapers. After the baby out grows them, they make good rags. Buy what you think your family will need. Remember, there may be no modern methods of birth control available.

Toilet paper - Stock what you consider practical. However, remember that for most of human history, toilet paper was not available. While it seems like a necessity in today's world, many other items have a higher priority for your survival. In some South American countries, they use sanitary washcloths. You will need three to five washcloths a day for each family member. After they are used, place them in a closed container full of soapy water. The cloths need to be washed once a day and dried in the sun. The sun helps to sanitize them.

Old magazines, corncobs and leaves have all been used in the past in place of toilet paper. Be sure you avoid poison oak, poison ivy and other irritants.

Dental hygiene - The condition of your teeth affects your overall health. Keep flossing and brushing. An improvised toothbrush can be easily made. Take a twig from a tree (willow or poplar is best). Sharpen one end to use for picking your teeth. Chew on the other end and use the fibers as a brush.

Sun washing clothes - If you have a real water shortage, shake your clothes out and spread them out in the full sun. The more the clothes are exposed to sun, the better. Sun washed clothing will feel cleaner and smell better. The ultraviolet radiation will kill off the bacteria that live in your sweat and dead skin cells. Do not forget to sun wash your sleeping bags and bedding.

Human waste - A temporary toilet can be made out of a five gallon bucket and one of the toilet seats from your home If you have plastic bags to line the bucket with, it is easier to dispose of the waste. Keep a can of wood ash, lime or other disinfectant by your improvised toilet to sprinkle over your waste. This helps to keep the smell down and the insects away. Cover the toilet when it is not in use. The waste can be disposed of by burying or burning. The problem with burning is that it takes a lot of fuel. Burying works well, but you have several things to consider.

How close is the nearest water? The U.S. Forest Service advises you to be at least 200 feet from a stream or well when you bury your waste. Consider the slope of the land and, if possible, bury the waste down slope from your water source. Remember, when it rains, you do not want the water to drain through your waste disposal area into your water source. When you bury waste, cover it with at least 18 to 24 inches of dirt.

If you are without normal sewage facilities for a long period, you may have to improvise them. Dig a slit trench 18 inches wide, 4 feet long and at least 4 feet deep. Rig up a privacy partition around it. You can use almost anything from brush, scrap lumber or old sheets etc. Since you will have to squat over the trench, you will need something to hang on to. Install a couple of posts within easy reach, you can even run a rope between them for additional support. Provide something to wipe with and wood ashes to cover the waste and you are in business.

Worms - These are something that most of us have not had to face in recent years. In many foreign counties, they are still quite common. Poor sanitation is the biggest reason for their spread. Worms are spread when people relieve themselves on the ground. The feces may contain roundworm eggs. Even if someone cleans the area, some eggs may remain in the ground. Roundworm eggs can remain infectious for many months. When children or adults contact the contaminated soil, the worms may infect them. Young children are particularly susceptible, since they often play or crawl on the ground.

Rodents and insects - Fleas, ticks, cockroaches, bedbugs, tapeworms, rats and mice are problems that our ancestors dealt with on a daily basis. They all are potential disease carriers. In a long-term emergency, they would become our problems. In planning your storage, you need to consider these issues. Your storage should include old-fashioned rat and mousetraps, rat poison, insect sprays and repellents. In addition, Chapter 8 Miscellaneous Recipes includes some old-fashioned insect repellants.

Flies are also responsible for the spread of disease. They like feeding on feces and can travel long distances. Flies have spikes on their legs, so particles of whatever they feed on are carried with them. If the flies are feeding on the feces of someone suffering from a diarrhea disease such as gastroenteritis, these particles may pass the disease on to others. The fly's next meal is quite likely to be on human food. So bits of feces are left behind on food or drink which is then eaten by people. The disease is then passed on.

Many of us routinely use air conditioning and do not often open our windows, so our window screens are not well maintained. If you intend to shelter in place consider maintaining your screens as part of your emergency preparations and do not forget the fly swatters.

In a survival situation hygiene is more important than normal; you cannot afford to get sick. Wash whenever you can and keep your food preparation areas as clean as possible. Keep your dishes, pots and pans clean. Clean sand can be used as an improvised scouring powder

PROPER DISPOSAL OF GARBAGE AND RUBBISH

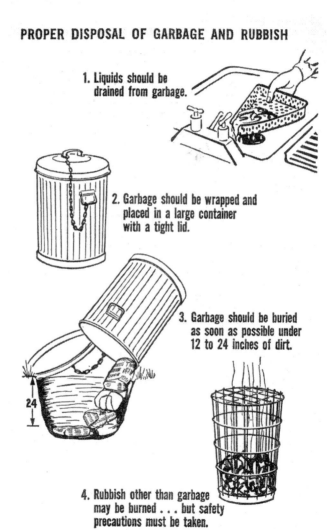

1. Liquids should be drained from garbage.

2. Garbage should be wrapped and placed in a large container with a tight lid.

3. Garbage should be buried as soon as possible under 12 to 24 inches of dirt.

24

4. Rubbish other than garbage may be burned . . . but safety precautions must be taken.

Chapter 7 - 72-Hour Kits

Everybody from Homeland Security to the American Red Cross advises you to have a 72-hour kit. They all have lists of suggested supplies. After reading their lists, I feel that they are all on the weak side. I operate on the assumption that whatever happens will occur at midnight on the coldest, wettest night of the year. If you are prepared for this, anything less will be easy.

Before you start on your kit, I want you to stop and think about how much you intend to spend. A common excuse is "I cannot afford it." If that is your excuse, look at the next homeless person you see. How much do you think his gear cost him? It may not look fancy, but it is keeping him alive. He is not just looking at 72 hours; his kit is his whole life. Do not hesitate to improvise, go to flea markets, thrift shops or garage sales. Some great equipment has been found in them for peanuts.

Each family member should have his or her own kit. They should be personalized for their needs. Kits should be kept at a central location that everyone is familiar with. Inspect your kit at least twice a year. Check children's clothing for proper fit.

A 72-hour kit needs to meet your three most important needs: food, water and warmth. Other than maybe special medical requirements, these are the most important requirements for keeping you alive.

Three days supply of food - Your needs will be determined by the size and age of your family and their personal needs. Remember that it always helps to have extra food. If you have to utilize your kit, you will be under a lot of stress. This is not a good time to skimp on food. You should plan for 2000 to 3000 calories a day.

Suggested items include MRE's (Meals Ready to Eat). MRE's are packaged military meals that have a good shelf life if kept in a cool spot. They are a complete meal including main course, dessert, snacks, drink powder and plastic utensils. They can be eaten cold, directly out of the package. No water is required for this preparation.

According to the U.S. Government, the shelf life of MRE's is as follows:
120 degrees - 1 month
110 degrees - 5 months
100 degrees - 22 months
90 degrees - 55 months
80 degrees - 76 months
70 degrees - 100 months
60 degrees - 130 months

Commercial freeze-dried or dehydrated, individually packaged meals are available at most sporting goods stores. The plus side is that they are convenient, nutritious, tasty and lightweight. The downsides are they require water to prepare and they are expensive.

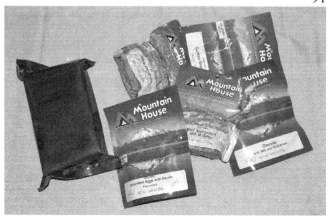

Military MRE on left, Mountain house meals from their "Just in Case" Unit on right.

The "Just in Case" Unit consists of 21 meals, including breakfasts, lunches and dinners. It provides all the food for a 72-hour kit for two people. The Mountain House meals have a seven-year shelf life at 75 degrees or less.

Canned food – meats, tuna, sardine, fruits, vegetables, chili, etc., all are good choices. The downside is their weight and the need to rotate.

Top Ramen Noodles - They need to be rotated often, are not well packaged (bugs can get in). Pack them in plastic Ziploc bags. They require water to prepare. The plus side is they are light and cheap.

Granola Bars or Power Bars, hard candy, fruit bars or fruit rolls, dried fruit and trail mix, etc., are all good products. However, you have to remember to rotate them, particularly anything with nuts. The oil in the nuts will turn rancid.

Lifeboat rations, or ration bars, provide approximately 1200 calories per day. Many of the prepackage 72 hour kits contain these type of bars. They are sold in 2400 and 3600 calorie packages and can be broken into 400-calorie sections. A meal is one 400-calorie section. Their taste is not too bad. Depending on the brand, they taste like lemon butter cookies or shortbread. The bars consist mainly of flour and sugar fortified with vitamins.

The rations will keep you alive, but you will be hungry and unhappy. Still there are some advantages to lifeboat ration bars. They will withstand long periods of heat and freezing temperatures. The bars are compact, lightweight and are packaged to withstand rough conditions. Because they are so inexpensive, I would double the rations if these were my choice.

Cooking utensils - My personal choice is the stainless steel U.S. military surplus mess kit. They are inexpensive, sturdy and reasonably lightweight. The US stainless steel knife, fork and spoon set make a good companion. There are many good commercial backpack cooking sets available at most sporting goods stores for a bit more money. It is recommended that you avoid aluminum cooking sets and plastic silverware. Plastic silverware is useless for cooking over an open fire.

Water- A good combination is a pair of US military surplus 1-quart canteens and covers. As an accessory, you can purchase a military surplus cup and a small stove. Both will fit inside the canteen cover. The canteen nests inside them. The stove works with military heat tabs that are readily available. One heat tab will boil a cup of water. Canteen covers have a pocket for water purification tablets. These components can be purchased at most military surplus stores and many of the suppliers listed in the Reference Section.

There are many good commercial water bladders, canteens and hydration backpacks on the market. Just be able to carry at least 2 quarts of water and have a method to purify more. If you live in a desert area and are physically able, you may want to carry 4 quarts or more of water. With canteens, you have many options; canteens can be improvised from water or juice bottles stuffed into an improvised bag.

Water can be purchased in small four-ounce foil packs that are manufactured for use in lifeboats. These have a shelf life of approximately four to five years. If you choose to carry these, remember you that need a gallon of water a day. There is 128 fluid ounces in a US gallon.

From left to right: 1-quart US canteen, bottle of water purification tablets, stove and canteen cup with heat tabs in front, canteen cover. Canteen fully assembled includes everything but the heat tabs (fuel). The purification tablets fit in pouch on the right side of the canteen cover.

Water purification - There are many suitable methods of water purification for a 72-hour kit. Chemical tablets or water filters are best. Boiling or SODIS both work well, but takes too much time if you need to evacuate.

Aquamira, Micropur and Portable Aqua all manufacture water purifications tablets containing chlorine dioxide that kills bacteria, viruses and cysts, including Giardia and Cryptosporidium. Chlorine dioxide does not discolor water, nor does it give water an unpleasant taste like iodine. They have a four to five year shelf life; check the expiration date on the packaging. While chlorine dioxide is the best product on the market, it has one downside. Some of the tablets require a 4-hour reaction time prior to drinking. Chlorine dioxide water treatment drops manufactured by Aquamira only require a fifteen-minute reaction time.

Portable Aqua iodine tablets come 50 per bottle. They have a 4-year shelf life but only 6 months after the seal is broken. One tablet per quart is a minimum water treatment. It is inexpensive and can be found in the camping section of almost any large discount or grocery store. Iodine will leave a taste in the water.

Polar Pure is an iodine crystal base product It is more expensive and harder to find than Portable Aqua (check the suppliers in the Reference Section). The advantage of Polar Pure is that it has no shelf life, and according to the instructions, a bottle will disinfect 2000 quarts of water. The disadvantage is that if you consumed that much iodine you may have medical complications.

Povidone 10% solution, normally sold under the name Betadine, is commonly found in most first aid kits. It will disinfect water; use 8-10 drops in clear water, up to 16 drops in turbid water. Portable Aqua Iodine tables, Polar Pure and povidone cause a slight taste in the water. The taste will not hurt you.

Warning - Pregnant or nursing women or persons with thyroid problems should not drink water disinfected with iodine. Prolonged use of iodine can cause medical problems in some people. In addition, some people who are allergic to shellfish are allergic to iodine.

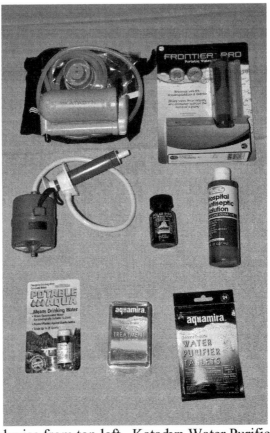

Clockwise from top left, Katadyn Water Purifier, Frontier Pro by aquamira, povidone 10% solution (Betadine), Polar Pure, Water purifier Tablets and Water treatment Drops by aquamira, Portable Aqua Tablets, an a First Need water purifier.

Warning - Iodine will not reliably kill Giardia and Cryptosporidium.

Water filters - First Need, Katadyn and Aquamira make excellent water purifiers. They have a large selection of sizes and price ranges. Choose the size that fits your family. The Frontier Pro by Aquamira is currently being used by the US Military. It is small, compact, efficient and reasonably priced There are other brands on the market that are just as good, but I have tried these three brands and can recommend them. If you decide to purchase a different brand, make sure it will eliminate Giardia and Cryptosporidium. Many of the products on the market are filters and not purifiers; this means that they may not filter all dangerous bacteria out of the water. Read the specifications.

Matches and Cigarette lighters are the fire starters most people are familiar with. They are readily available and every home probably has a few books or boxes of matches stuck in a drawer somewhere. Matches are handy, cheap, store well and are easy to use. The problem is not with the matches, it is with us. We all like to think we can start a fire with one match. Try it, most people will be surprised at how hard it is to start a fire in good conditions with dry wood. Starting one on a cold windy night with wet wood takes practice. Most waterproof match cases only hold about a dozen strike anywhere matches. Store extra matches; they will be good to trade with those who do not practice fire starting. I recommend the strike anywhere kitchen matches.

Top row: Commercial fire starters and military heat tabs. Second row: cigarette lighters, waterproof match case and matches. Third row: BlastMatch, Strike Force and a Speedy Sharp. Fourth Row: a Sparkie, magnesium block and flint, and two flints, one on key ring.

Military heat tabs or other prepared fire starters belong in every kit. You can purchase them through the suppliers in the Reference Section or make your own. They can be as simple as cotton balls impregnated with Vaseline. An old 35 mm film can makes a great storage container for them. Another fire starter is to melt wax in a double boiler and add sawdust until the mixture starts to become stiff. Then pour the melted mixture into the bottom of old egg cartons and let it harden. Because of the fire hazard, it is best to do this chore outside. Once the mixture has hardened, you can cut the carton in twelve sections and carry a couple with you. You can break a section up and use as much as needed.

There are many commercial fire starters such as a block of magnesium and a flint. You see this all the time on the television show, "Survivor." They are available in most sporting goods sections. If you take the time to learn to use them they work well, but they do take two hands. Scrape some of the magnesium into your tinder pile before creating your sparks. I use the Speedy Sharp for both scraping the magnesium and making the sparks. The Speedy Sharp also serves double duty by sharpening knives.

Innovations such as the Gerber Strike Force and the BlastMatch are improved fire starters. The BlastMatch can be used with one hand. The one that best suits my requirements is the Sparkie from Ultimate Survival. It weights less than 1 oz and can be used one-handed. I always carry a small flint on my key chain for backup. Do not forget to practice; flints are hard to use.

Backpack Stoves

From left to right: Coleman fuel, propane and a Sierra stove.

There are many small backpack stoves on the market. The problem with most of them is fuel; you need to carry a flammable liquid or a propane bottle. The Sierra stove is one of the exceptions; it burns wood. It utilizes a small fan to create a forge like effect. The fan requires one double A battery. You can carry a rechargeable double A battery and a solar charger that only weighs a few ounces. If your flashlight uses double A batteries they should also be rechargeable.

Sanitation - If you are forced to evacuate you may not have much choice about where you end up staying, but you do have some say about the conditions you live in. Keep your space as clean as possible. Keep yourself clean; it will help your morale as well as your health. Be sure and put the following items in your kit:.

Toilet paper - Store it in a plastic bag to keep it clean and dry.
Bar of soap - Store in plastic soap dish or zip lock bag.
Towel - Small hand towel
Feminine supplies - As needed
Personal items - Medication as needed
Toothbrush and toothpaste
Insect repellant - The type may vary depending on where you live.
Sun Screen - You do not need the additional problems of bad sunburn.
Shaving gear
A comb

Warmth and Shelter

Sleeping bags - A good sleeping bag is the best choice for warmth and comfort. There are many good sleeping bags on the market, but the best is probably the Wiggy's. They are a bit on the expensive side, but how much is a good night's sleep worth? Whatever type of bag you choose here are some tips to help you:

Goose Down is more expensive, lighter, compresses easier, warmer by weight, more durable and long-lived. However, if it gets wet, it is useless. In extreme cold, your body releases moisture as you sleep, so a down bag can get wet from the inside even when it is protected from the outside elements.

Some of the newer insulations such as Lamilite or Polarguard 3D will keep you warm when wet

Check the stitching; the tubes should overlap so that the stitching does not go all the way through the bag wall creating cold spots.

Make sure the bag has a sturdy zipper and a draft tube along the entire length of zipper.

Consider an outer Gore-Tex or other water repellant shell for your bag. However, be sure that the shell you purchase will breathe enough to allow body moisture to escape.

Mummy bags are lightweight, the most efficient for warmth and takes less room in your pack.

Remember, you have to carry it. Think about the weight.

I often see good quality sleeping bags in garage sales for pennies on the dollar.

If you cannot get a sleeping bag, the next best choice is a 100% wool army blanket. Wool retains a lot of its warmth when wet. They are a bit on the heavy side, but are inexpensive. Surplus blankets are available for $10-15, and there are always thrift shops.

Space blanket - They are for emergency use, only when you have no other choices. A friend used one as a cover for his sleeping bag in near zero weather. It caused enough condensation to make his bedding very damp. They are small, light and are designed to help your body retain its own natural heat. In cold weather, they may help to keep you alive, but you will not be comfortable. On the plus side, they make a fair ground cover; they will shed water and make a good windbreak. If you decide to go with a space blanket, look for the space blanket bivy sack. This is like a sleeping, bag although made of the same material as a space blanket.

Rain poncho - In my opinion one of your most important survival items. I like the military surplus ones; they are sturdier than most civilian models. A poncho can keep you and your equipment dry while hiking. With a little light line, they make a good rain shelter over your bed or a good ground cover.

Large trash bags - I always shove a couple of trash bags in my 72-hour kit. They can be used for anything from improvising a sleeping bag to a poncho. For a sleeping bag, stuff them with old newspapers or other insulation. Just remember to leave the top open so they can breathe or you will wake up wet from condensation. A rain poncho can be made by cutting a hole for your head and pulling it on like a sweater. If you are wearing incorrect footwear, a piece of plastic between your socks and shoes will help keep your feet warm.

A piece of 8' x 10' plastic makes a good improvised shelter. You can make a good solid anchor by folding a small rock into the corner and tying a light line around it. Put the plastic over a tree branch or a rope stretched between two trees, then anchor the corners down with the light lines you have tied around the rocks and you have a good shelter.

Miscellaneous

Battery power or solar power radio- Some of the solar and hand crank radios currently on the market are excellent. A radio provides you with knowledge that might save your life. Check the references for a good source.

Knives -A good, sturdy high quality knife is one of your most important tools. Avoid cheap foreign brands. Either a folding or straight bladed knife will work; the blade does not need to be over 4 inches long. If you can afford it, consider multi tools like the Leatherman Wave. It is my personal choice. Do not forget a small sharpening stone.

Flashlight - Yon need a good flashlight. There are many good quality LCD models currently on the market. Most use AA batteries. Do not forget the spare batteries. Rotate them periodically. An alternative is to use rechargeable batteries and carry a small solar charger. Beware of cheap foreign imitations.

Rope - An excellent choice is a 50 ft. hank of surplus military parachute line (550 cord). This is very strong for its size. It is made up of numerous small strands of heavy thread inside of a fabric tube. The individual threads can be pulled out and used for sewing or repairing equipment.

Shovel - Include a surplus military entrenching tool and cover, or a small shovel for burying waste. The Glock entrenching shovel is an excellent choice. There are many cheap imitation entrenching tools on the market that will break with hard use, so go to a reputable supplier.

Backpack -You need a good backpack or other bag to carry your 72-hour kit. There are many good packs both civilian and military on the market. Get a pack that fits you, load your gear and take it out for a good hike (ten or more miles). I personally like a backpack with an external frame. Make sure yours has a good padded waist belt and distributes the weight between your shoulders and hips.

If you cannot afford a good backpack, try looking in garage sales and thrift stores. You can improvise one out of old luggage, duffel bags, daypacks, etc. If you have to evacuate on foot, try not to carry your pack. Load your pack into the kid's wagon, onto a bicycle, into a wheelbarrow, golf cart or any other wheeled device you can think of. You can always strap it to your back, if your carrier breaks or the terrain gets too rough.

Things to consider when buying a backpack
(information from Freeze Dry Guy):

Comfort
Load bearing capability (how much weight do
  you have to carry)
Cost
Color
Ruggedness
Versatility

Civilian Backpacks

Advantages
Usually more advanced
Normally very comfortable
Lighter than military

Disadvantages
Usually not as rugged as military
Often much more expensive
Fewer places to hang gear on outside of pack
Often times available only in bright colors (do you
  want to be seen?)

Military Backpacks

Advantages:
Much less expensive than civilian
Widely available
Very rugged
Subdued colors
More places to hang equipment on outside of pack

Generally, more pockets for storing gear, easier
to access more items of equipment
Some packs can be made quite comfortable with
certain after market modifications

Disadvantages
Often times not as comfortable as civilian packs
Usually heavier than civilian packs
Often not as well designed as civilian packs

Clothing - Your clothing should be appropriate to
the climate zone in which you reside. They should
include a warm jacket, hat, and gloves. Do not
forget good footwear, preferably boots with 2 extra
pair of heavy socks. The boots should be
comfortable and well broken in. The clothing
should be subdued in color.

Photos - Every pack especially children's should
contain a family photo. If you are separated, having
a picture to show others is worth a thousand words.
This is particularly important for young children
that have trouble communicating.

Cash - One hundred dollars in small bills,
preferably one-dollar bills.

Important papers - Do not forget your important
papers for example, insurance, identification,
passports and financial, etc.

First aid kit - It should contain a minimum of the
following items. Packed in a waterproof container
if possible.

Surgical dressing, approx. 4" x 6"
Band-aids assorted sizes
Gauze pad 4" four each
Gauze pad 2" four each
Adhesive tape ¾"
First aid book
Vaseline
Triangular bandage
Antiseptic
Anti-diarrhea medicine
Aspirin and acetaminophen
Calamine lotion
Cotton swabs
Ace bandage, 3"
Moleskin for blisters
Sunscreen
Mosquito repellant
Prescription medicine as needed

Chapter 8 - Miscellaneous Recipes

Cooking wheat cereal and saving fuel

In a saucepan bring 1 part wheat to two parts water to a boil. Remove it from the heat and cover. Let it sit for at least 10 hours.

Whole wheat bread recipe

6 cups warm water
2 tablespoons yeast
½-cup honey
Tablespoon salt
18 cups of flour

Dissolve the yeast in 1 teaspoon of honey and a ¼-cup of warm water. The water should feel about the temperature you would use for a baby's bottle. If it is too hot, it will probably kill the yeast. Wait five minutes; if the mixture foams and smells yeasty, the yeast is active. (This is called proofing the yeast. If you are using rapid rise yeast, you do not need to proof the yeast.) Add the rest of the honey, salt and water.

Stir in 12 cups of flour. Pile 4 cups of flour on mixing board. Take about 2 cups of dough and place on pile of flour. Knead in just enough flour so that the dough is no longer sticky. Repeat this until all the flour is added. Put the remaining two cups of flour on the board and knead all the dough for 10 minutes.

Place the dough in a greased bowl and set in an unheated oven with a bowl of water heated to about 140 degrees. Place the water under the bowl of dough and place a damp towel over the dough. With the help of the humidity the dough should double in about 45 minutes. Divide the dough into greased pans. Let the dough rise until it doubles again. Bake at 350 for 1 hour.

Cracked wheat

1-cup cracked wheat (coarsely ground)
3 cups water
Salt to taste

Mix cracked wheat and salt into boiling water and cook in double boiler for 15 to 20 minutes. Pre soaking the wheat can shorten the cooking time.

Hard tack

4 cups wheat flour
Water
Salt

Mix flour, salt, and water until the dough is moist throughout. Form the dough into 4 inch squares ½ inch thick. Place on greased cookie tray. Take a fork and punch holes in the squares. Cook them until they are completely dry. There should be no moisture left in them.

Stored in paper or cloth bags and protected from

insects, they should last a year or more. This is the
famous hard tack used in the civil war. You will
want to soak the squares prior to eating, if you want
to keep your teeth.

Wild yeast

1-quart warm potato water
½ yeast cake
1 teaspoon salt
2 tablespoons sugar
2 cups white or whole wheat flour

Mix the ingredients. Place mixture in a warm spot
to rise until ready to use for baking. Keep a small
amount of the yeast to use for a starter for the next
batch. Between uses, keep the yeast starter in the
refrigerator, or keep as cool as possible until a few
hours prior to use.

Add the same ingredients with the exception of
yeast to the wild yeast starter before your next
baking. By keeping the yeast starter live, yeast can
be kept on hand indefinably.

Sour dough starter

2 cups white or whole-wheat flour
2 cups warm water
2 teaspoons honey or sugar

Mix all the ingredients well. Place the mixture in
an uncovered glass or crockery jar and place in a

warm room. Allow the mixture to ferment for 5 days, stirring several times a day. Stirring will aerate the mixture and allow air to activate the yeast. Small bubbles will rise to the top and it give off a yeasty odor.

After each use, the starter will need to be fed. Replace the amount of starter you used with equal parts of flour and water. In 24 hours, the yeast will be reformed and be ready for use again. Store the unused portion in a glass or crockery jar. Keep the mixture in a refrigerator or the coolest possible place. Just prior to use, activate the mixture by adding 2 to 3 tablespoons of flour and the same amount of water. Sour dough starter can replace all or part of the commercial yeast in a recipe.

Sour dough biscuits

1-1/2 cup sifted flour
2 teaspoons baking powder
1/4 teaspoon baking soda (if starter is quite sour, use 1/2 teaspoon soda)
1/2 teaspoon salt
1/4 cup soft butter
1 cup starter

Sift the dry ingredients together. Mix in the butter. Then add the starter and mix well. Place the dough on a lightly floured board. Knead lightly until smooth and elastic. Roll dough 1/2" thick, cut with a floured cutter. Place biscuits in a greased pan and brush with butter. Let the dough rise one hour in a warm place. Then bake in hot oven at 425 degrees for 20 minutes. Serve hot. This recipe makes about one dozen biscuits.

Sour Dough Hot Cakes

1 cup starter
2 cups flour
2 cups milk
1 teaspoon salt
2 teaspoons baking soda
3 tablespoons melted shortening
2 tablespoons sugar
2 eggs

About 12 hours before serving hot cakes, mix starter, flour, milk and salt. Let stand in a cheesecloth covered bowl in a warm place. Immediately before cooking, add eggs, soda, shortening and sugar to the batter in the bowl. Mix well and bake on griddle. For thinner cakes, add more milk. Makes about 30 cakes.

Egg substitute

Combine 1 teaspoon unflavored gelatin with 3 tablespoons cold water and stir until dissolved. Add 2 tablespoons boiling water and mix. This will substitute for one egg. Decrease the water in your recipes to allow for the extra water in the egg substitute.

Homemade baking powder

½ teaspoon cream of tartar
¼ teaspoon cornstarch or arrowroot
¼ teaspoon baking soda

Mix together. It makes one teaspoon baking powder.

Corn syrup

Mix one cup sugar and two cups water. Cook until the mixture is thick. Substitute for corn syrup.

Cornmeal mush

1/2 cup cornmeal
2-3/4 cups Water
3/4 teaspoon Salt

Mix cornmeal into boiling water, stirring constantly.
Add salt and cook for about half an hour.
Serve with milk and sugar.

Cornmeal Jonny cake

Combine 1 cup stone ground white cornmeal
1 teaspoon sugar
1/2 teaspoon salt
1- 3/4 cups milk

In a large bowl, combine cornmeal, sugar and salt. Stir in ¾ cups of milk. This should make a thin batter. Drop batter by the tablespoon-full onto a hot well-oiled iron griddle and cook the cakes over low heat for 4 or 5 minutes until underside is browned. Turn the cakes over and cook them for 5 minutes, or until brown. Serve the Jonny cakes very hot with butter and syrup.

Preparation of Ground Acorns

Many of the Native Americans used acorns as a staple in their diet. Acorns taste like a cross between hazelnuts and sunflower seeds and makes first-rate flatbread. In a long-term emergency, this is an excellent way to supplement your diet.

Gather several handfuls of acorns. All acorns in the United States are edible. Some contain more tannin than others, but leaching will remove the tannin from all of them. Shell the acorns with a nutcracker, a hammer or a rock. The meat should be yellowish, not black and dusty (insects).

Grind the shelled acorns. If you do not have a grinder, crush them, a few at a time on a hard boulder with a smaller stone, Indian style. Do this until all the acorns are crushed into a crumbly paste.

Leach (wash) them. Line a big colander with a dishtowel or other clean cloth and fill with the ground acorns. Slowly pour water through the colander, stirring with one hand, for about five minutes. A lot of brown liquid will come out. This is the tannin. When the water runs clear, stop and taste a little. If the meal is not bitter, you have washed it enough.

If you do not have a colander, tie the meal up in a clean cloth and soak it in buckets of clean drinking water, until it passes the taste test.

Drain the mash, or squeeze out as much water as you can, with your hands. One warning: do not let wet acorn meal lie about for hours or it will mold. Use the ground acorn mash right away because it turns dark when left out in the heat.

Acorn flour will not rise by itself. Indian breads were small, thin cakes baked before the fire on large, reflecting rocks. If you mix it with flour containing gluten in a ratio of 1 to 1, it will rise. Acorn flour can be used as a thickener for soups and stews.

Uses for the brown acorn water

Save the brown water from the first leaching. The brown water should be kept as cool as possible. Over time, a mold may form on top of the water and you will need to boil the water again to kill the mold. The brown water may be used in any of the following ways:

Laundry Detergent: Two cups of the brown water can be used as laundry detergent for one load of clothes. Your clothes will smell very good but lighter colors (and whites) will take on a tan tint.

Traditional Herbal Home Remedies: The brown acorn water has medicinal properties.

Wash the skin to ease the discomfort of skin rashes, burns, and small cuts.
Externally it can be used to treat hemorrhoids.

Hide Tanning: Tannic acid or brown acorn water is used in the process of animal hide tanning. Soak the clean, scraped animal hides in the brown water. The name tanning comes from the term tannic acid, which was originally used to tan hides.

Indian acorn griddlecakes

2 cups acorn meal
1/2 teaspoon salt
3/4 cup water

Combine the ingredients and beat to a stiff batter. Let stand for one hour. Heat one tablespoon of fat or oil in a frying pan. Drop batter into pan to form cakes about three to four inches across. Brown cakes slowly on both sides. These cakes can be stored for several days.

Toothpaste

Equal amounts of salt and powdered sage leaves make good toothpaste.

Cures for Insects and Rodents

If skunks get into your garage or under your house, throw a handful of mothballs into the area. They hate the smell and will leave almost immediately.

A piece of cloth well saturated with cayenne pepper can be used to plug rat and mouse holes.

Cockroaches and ants have a dislike of cayenne pepper.

Sassafras oil drops will drive ants away. Put a few drops on the shelves.

Branches of elder bush hung in the house will help keep flies away. They do not like the odor.

Eucalyptus tree leaves placed in a closet will keep moths away.

African daisies (pyrethrum) dried and powdered are an excellent insecticide. They are the basis for many modern commercial insect repellants.

Insect do not like bay leaves. Make little cloth bags of them and place in cupboards or drawers to keep insects away. Bay trees grow wild in many areas of the country.

Matches and Fires

Waterproof your matches by melting wax into a small bowl and dipping about half the length of a match into the melted wax.

Save the grease and fat from your cooking. Pour it over shredded paper or tinder to make improvised fire starters.

Kindling can be dried out in your solar oven.

When you light a campfire, look for dried resin or pitch wood. Scrape the pitch or resin into your tinder, this makes a good fire starter. Pine trees seem to be the best source of resin or pitch.

Look under downed timber for dry punk (rotten) wood. Even when it is raining, you may find dry wood.

Chapter 9 - Improvised Equipment

Under this heading, you will find some things that are handy to have and some ideas on how to improvise.

Keeping your food cool helps to prolong its edible life and makes many things more appetizing. Many things will work; your useless electric refrigerator is well insulated and can be effective as a cooler. Picnic coolers are very useful; they can be set in the ground and covered up, but be wary of animals.

An iceless refrigerator is simple and cheap to make and will keep food cool. At one time, these were common all over the South Western United States. They work best in a dry climate.

Instructions For Making an Iceless Refrigerator

   Make a wooden or PVC pipe frame approximately 48 -58 inches high by 12 -18 inches wide and deep. Cover the outside with a wire screen or hardware cloth. The covering should be something that preferably will not rust and will keep insects out. The top should be screen and the bottom solid. Make a door for one side and hang it on hinges or leather straps. Use a hook or a button for a latch.

The inside shelves can be fixed or adjustable and should be made of a frame covered with wire fencing such as chicken wire. This will allow airflow.

Paint the wooden frames with whatever type of paint you have available. If you do not have paint, use linseed or cooking oil and give it time to dry.

Next, make a cover of burlap, flannel, or any heavy, coarse, water absorbent cloth. Put the smooth side of the material on the outside. Attach the cover around the top of the frame with nails, buttons, etc. Leave a flap for the door to open.

Place a 2-4 inch deep pan on top of the frame. Sew strips of cloth to the top of the cover and extend them into the top pan. They are to act as a wick to draw water into the cover.

Place a second pan under the bottom of the frame and make sure the bottom of the cover reaches into it.

Stand the refrigerator in a shady place where there is good airflow. The refrigerator works when you fill both pans with water. The water wicks into the cover and saturates it. The airflow causes an evaporative action similar to a swamp cooler. You can jump-start the refrigerator by first pouring water over the cover. The faster the rate of evaporation gets, the cooler the temperature.

A collapsible variation of this refrigerator was often used at campsites. It was hung from a tree branch out of the reach of animals.

Iceless Refrigerator

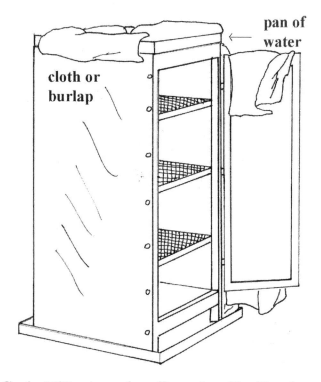

pan of water ←

cloth or burlap

Grain Mills- A good quality grain mill will make your life much easier. There is currently a disagreement between proponents of stone ground and metal-jawed mills. Some feel that the heat generated by the stones causes a loss of nutrition.

I feel that either is a good choice. Before you purchase a mill, try it. You might be surprised at the amount of strength it takes to use it. I knew someone who powered theirs with a bicycle. If you intend to do this get the parts now and perfect it before you need it.

Here is a diagram of an alternate method of cracking your grain. This is a method of last resort, it is slow and hard work.

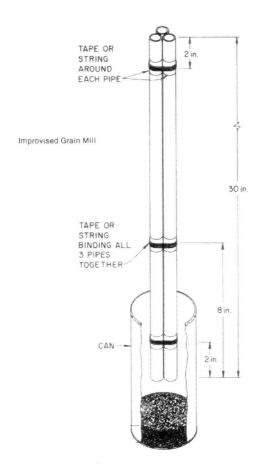

TAPE OR
STRING
AROUND
EACH PIPE

2 in.

Improvised Grain Mill

30 in.

TAPE OR
STRING
BINDING ALL
3 PIPES
TOGETHER

8 in.

CAN

2 in.

Place 1 to 2 inches of grains in the can and use the pipes to crack the grain. This will not make fine grain flour, but just cracking it will save you a lot of cooking and soaking time.

Solar ovens

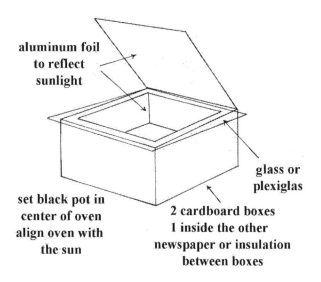

The outside dimensions should be approximately 24 inches square. The inner box should be approximately 20 inches square. The space in between the two boxes should be filled with insulation. This can consist of newspaper or cardboard. Line the inside and the top reflector with aluminum foil and put a lid of glass or Plexiglas and you are ready to cook.

Rocket stove

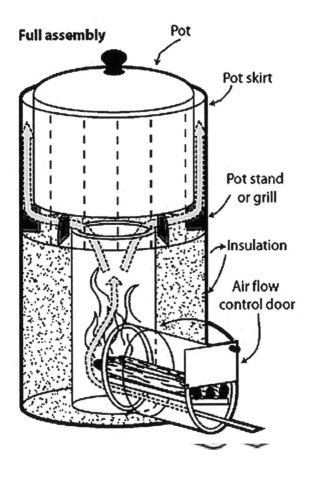

Full assembly

Pot

Pot skirt

Pot stand
or grill

Insulation

Air flow
control door

A five-gallon bucket works well for the outer
container.

126

Winiarski / Aprovecho rocket stove

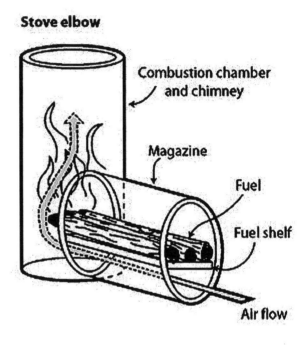

A four-inch pipe works well for the combustion chamber and chimney. I have seen these made using stovepipe, but I prefer something a little heavier. Dirt or crushed lava rock makes a good insulation. The fuel shelf can be made out of an old tin can. Using the same principal, you can improvise these stoves out of brick or tile.

Do not forget the old pioneer standby - a good axe.

They cleared fields and built houses with not much more. If you are planning on burning wood, have the tools to cut it. Do not depend on your chain saw. The same principle applies if you are planning a garden: shovels, spades, forks, rakes, etc. You cannot think of everything: just do your best. And remember, if you have anything extra, you can always trade.

Chapter 10 - Some Last Thoughts

It is my hope that you will never have to use the preparedness foods, tools and ideas that are discussed in this book. However, if such an occasion occurs, it is my hope that this book will make your life a little bit easier.

A few things to remember that might help you stay alive are.

Do not brag to your neighbors and friends about your storage and preparations. If you are in a position, where it is impossible to keep this information a secret, consider moving your storage to a safe location in your immediate area (a location you can walk too).

Be careful who you trust, choose your friends wisely. When people are betrayed, it is normally by someone they trusted.

How much you choose to help your friends and neighbors is up to you and your conscience. You are the ant and they are the grasshoppers from the old fable. If you know that you will not be able to stand being a witness to the sufferings of those around you, you may want to consider continuing to expand your food storage and other supplies to help them.

One way of helping people is to trade food for work. Preparing and finding food and water will

consume most of your time. You can have needy
people help plant your garden, carry water, gather
acorns, etc.

 Learning how to grow a garden takes time. Plant a
small garden now. Learn how to compost. Do you
know what grows well in your area? How many
crops can you grow a year? The better gardener
you are now, may determine, how well you and
your family eat in the future.

Stock a good supply of vegetable seeds. Make sure
the seeds are non-hybrid seeds which allows you to
harvest your own seeds for future plantings. You
can purchase the seeds in sealed cans that will store
for about four years. These are available through
some of the suppliers mentioned in the Resources
Section.

If you have the land, plant a few fruit trees. They
take a few years to become productive. Learn how
to take maintain them.

 Plant some rose bushes. Rose hips are high in
Vitamin C, with about 1700 to 2000 mg per
100 grams of the dried product. This is one of the
richest plant sources of vitamin C. Rose hips also
contain vitamins D and E, essential fatty acids and
antioxidant flavonoids. Rose hip powder has been
used as a remedy for rheumatoid arthritis.

Rose hips are the berry-like seedpods of the rose
bush left behind after the bloom has died. We often

prune them off to encourage more flowers to bloom. If you leave the spent flowers on the rose bush at the end of the season, you should see these small, berry-sized, reddish to orange seed balls, left on the tips of the stems. These are the rose hips. They can be dried and used as a powder or made into tea.

A hard decision for many people is, how far to go in protecting their food. This is a decision only you can make. I have known people who are more than ready to shoot someone and others who say they will not do anything to protect their food, but will rely on the Lord.

The same thing applies to protecting your family. If you have firearms, will you use them? My personal opinion is that you do whatever is necessary to protect your family and friends. .

What kind of physical condition are you in? You may have to hike or exert yourself physically in an emergency. Conditioning is part of being prepared. Walk to the store, use your bike or go to the gym. Take advantage of the opportunities around you to keep yourself healthy and in shape.

When did you last go to the doctor or dentist? Keep your shots up to date. Do you have any cavities? The fewer medical problems you have, the better your chances of survival.

In an emergency, you may have to eat some things you are not use too. Some of the foods may be considered disgusting by normal standards. The rattraps you have in your storage may become a source of food. The dandelions you have been trying to get out of your lawn may be part of lunch. If you think about these conditions now and make up your mind to survive it will be easier later.

The suppliers in the Resource Section are ones that I have had some dealing with, or trusted friends have referred them to me.

The books that are included in the Resource Section are books that I have read or reviewed. Like any source, you will have to study the information and evaluate it for yourself.

In any survival situation the more knowledge you have, the more opinions you have. Study and learn before the emergency.

Remember, if you are prepared you shall not fear.

Reference Section

Suppliers

FREEZE DRY GUY   An excellent resource, one I
use personally and highly recommend.
P.O. Box 1476
Grass Valley, CA 95945
866.404.3663 (FOOD)
email: info@FreezeDryGuy.com
http://www.Freezedryguy.com
Freeze-dried and dehydrated foods and sleeping
bags, etc.

Emergency Essentials
Orem Store
216 E University Parkway
Orem, Utah 84058
1-801-222-9667
http://www.beprepared.com
All types of freeze dried and dehydrated foods and
other miscellaneous preparedness
supplies

Walton Feed, Inc.
135 North 10th Street
Montpelier, ID 83254
208-847-0465 or 800-847-0465
Fax: 208-847-0467
Email: info@waltonfeed.com
or rainydayfoods@yahoo.com
Dehydrated Foods and Food Storage

Major Surplus & Survival
435 W. Alondra
Gardena, CA, 90248
 800) 441-8855 - Toll Free
(310) 324-8855 - Direct
(310) 324-6909 - Fax Sales: Sales@MajorSurplus.com
Customer Support: CustomerCare@MajorSurplus.com
Food and preparedness supplies

Lehman's, Kidron, Ohio • USA
http://www.lehmans.com
1-877-438-5346
Lanterns, gaslights, and independent living supplies

BriteLyt, Inc.
9 BriteLyt, Inc.
9516 Lake Dr.
New Port Richey, FL. 34654
USA
Ph: 727-856-9245
Fax: 727-856-7715 516 Lake Dr
http://www.britelyt.com/
The distributor of BriteLyt lanterns
New Port Richey, FL. 346

Ranger Joe's
Distribution Center
325 Farr Rd
Columbus, GA 31907
(800) 247-4541
http://www.rangerjoes.com
Military, law enforcement and survival gear

Wisemen Trading and Supply USA
P 8971 Lentzville Rd.
Athens, AL 35614
contact@wisementrading.com
(256)-729-8868
Fax (256)-729-6788
Order Toll Free 1-888-891-841
http://www.wisementrading.com
They carry rural living/homesteading supplies,
preparedness/survival needs.
They are a good source of independent living
supplies and the Sierra stoves.

Blackhawk
1-800-694-5263
http://www.blackhawk.com
Military, law enforcement and survival gear

Blendtec - Blendtec.com   Look at the Marga Mill
1-800-253-6383
Local: 801-222-0888
Fax: 801-805-8585
Address
1206 South 1680 West
Orem, Utah 84058

Aquamira Technologies, Inc.
917 West 600 North
Logan, UT, 84321
877-324-5358 Phone
sales@aquamira.com
Water purification tables and filters

Food Preservation

Curing and Smoking Meats for Home Food Preservation
Literature Review and Critical Preservation Points
http://www.uga.edu/nchfp/publications/nchfp/lit_rev/cure_smoke_pres.html

National Center for Home Food Preservation
http://www.uga.edu/nchfp/
A helpful site on food preservation.

EAWAG Aquatic Research
http://www.sodis.ch/
Information on the SODIS method of water purification.

Cooking

Byron's - Introduction to Dutch Ovens
http://papadutch.home.comcast.net/~papadutch/dutch-oven-intro.htm

Ammunition and Firearms Accessories

Cheaper Than Dirt!
P.O. Box 162087
Fort Worth, TX 76161
1-800-559-0943
http://www.cheaperthandirt.com
Shooting supplies and some camping and first aid supplies.

MidwayUSA
CustomerService@MidwayUSA.com
1-800-243-3220
1-800-992-8312
5875 West Van Horn Tavern Rd.
Columbia, MO 65203-9274
Just about everything for Shooting, Reloading, and
Gunsmithing.

Midsouth Shooters Supply
770 Economy Dr
Clarksville, TN 37043
1-800-272-3000
1-931 553-8651
Fax 1-931 503-8037
mss@midsouthshooterssupply.com
http://www.midsouthshooterssupply.com

Natchez Shooters Supplies, Inc.
P.O. Box 182212
Chattanooga, TN 37422
1-800-251-7839
https://www.natchezss.com

Firearms Training Schools

Tactical Firearms Training Team —
Great firearms instruction. Go to their school
TFTT 16835 Algonquin St. #120 Huntington
Beach, CA 92649
http://www.tftt.com/
1-714-206-5168

Gunsite
2900 W. GUNSITE ROAD
PAULDEN, AZ. 86334
Phone: 928-636-4565
Fax: 928-636-1236
www.gunsite.com

Thunder Ranch®
96747 Hwy 140 East • Lakeview, Oregon 97630
541-947-4104
http://www.thunderranchinc.com

Books

Life After Doomsday by Bruce Clayton Ph.D.
Nuclear Warfare Survival

The Ship's Medicine Chest and Medical Aid at Sea by U S Public Health Service
This is a medical book designed for ships at sea,
that do not carry a Doctor.

Keeping the Harvest: Discover the Homegrown Goodness of Putting Up Your Own Fruits,
Vegetables & Herbs (Down-to-Earth Book)
by Nancy Chioffi and Gretchen Mead
This is an excellent book on the art of preserving
food.

Nuclear War survival Skills by Cresson H Kearny
The gold standard of books on nuclear warfare.

When all Hell Breaks Loose by Cody Lundin
Excellent book on self-reliance a good survival
guide.

How to Survive on Land and Sea
by Frank C. Craighead and John J. Craighead
This book is on living off the land and other
survival skills.

SAS Survival Handbook: How to Survive in the
Wild, in Any Climate, on Land or at Sea by John
Lofty Wiseman

Outdoor Safety and Survival
by Paul H. Risk
A good general text on outdoor survival

**Medicine: For Mountaineering & Other
Wilderness Activities** 5th Edition
by James A. Wilkerson
A good first aid book for backpackers

Emergency War Surgery: Third United States
Revision, 2004 (Textbooks of Military Medicine)
by Andy C. Szul, Lorraine B. Davis, and Walter
Reed Army Medical Center Borden Institute

Where There Is No Dentist by Murray Dickson
The book is available from Amazon.com

Where There Is No Doctor: A Village Health Care Handbook
by Jane Maxwell, Carol Thuman, David Werner, Carol Thuman and Jane Maxwell
Available from Amazon.com

Passport to Survival by Esther Dickey
Available at Amazon.com
Food storage and preparation

Skills for Survival by Esther Dickey
Available at Amazon.com
Miscellaneous Survival skills

The Complete Walker IV
by Colin Fletcher and Chip Rawlins

Earth Medicine, Earth Food
by Michael A. Weiner

Ditch Medicine: Advanced Field Procedures For Emergencies by Hugh Coffee

US Army Special Forces Medical Handbook:
United States Army Institute for Military Assistance
by US ARMY

Nature Bound Pocket Field Guide by Ron Dawson
Pacific Press Publishing Association
Boise, Idaho
An excellent compact book on survival an edible plants, which can be found in the United States.

So Easy To Preserve is a 375-page book with over 185 tested recipes, along with systematic instructions and in-depth information for both the new and experienced food preserver.
Office of Communications
117 Hoke Smith Annex
Cooperative Extension Service
The University of Georgia
Athens, GA 30602-1456:
Phone: (706) 542-2657
Email: cespub@uga.edu
Fax: (706) 542-0817

Army TM 5-690
Grounding and Bonding in Command, Control, Communications, Computer, Intelligence, Surveillance and Reconnaissance (C4ISR) Facilities
Department of the Army (CEMP)
Date published 15 February 2002
This books covers grounding for protection against EMP.
The book can be downloaded from the web site http://140.194.76.129/publications/armytm/tm5-690/

Survival Web Sites

Hoods Woods - http://www.survival.com
One of the finest survival instructors, he has excellent DVD's, VHS's, and a survival forum. The World Leader in Survival Instructional Videos.

Equipped to survive -
http://www.equippedtosurvive.com
Equipped To Survive® is the most comprehensive
online resource for independent reviews of survival
equipment and outdoors gear, as well as survival
and Search and Rescue information.

Solar

Free Sun Power - http://www.freesunpower.com/
Excellent site for improved solar systems

The Renewable Energy Handbook: A Guide to
Rural Energy Independence, Off-Grid, Sustainable
Living and Solar Power
by William H. Kemp

Real Goods - http://www.realgoods.com
This site is a source of solar, wind, and hydropower
equipment, including solar-powered devices for
camping.

Index

144

Notes

Made in the USA
Lexington, KY
17 March 2010